NEW YORK REVIEW BOOKS
CLASSICS

DOWN BELOW

LEONORA CARRINGTON (1917–2011) was born in Lancashire, England, to an industrialist father and an Irish mother. She was raised on fantastical folk tales told to her by her Irish nanny at her family's estate, Crookhey Hall. Carrington would be expelled from two convent schools before enrolling in art school in Florence. In 1937, a year after her mother gave her a book on surrealist art featuring Max Ernst's work, she met the artist at a party. Not long after, Carrington and the then-married Ernst settled in the south of France, where Carrington completed her first major painting, *The Inn of the Dawn Horse (Self-Portrait)*, in 1939. In the wake of Ernst's imprisonment by the Nazis, Carrington fled to Spain, where she suffered a nervous breakdown and was committed to a mental hospital in Madrid. She eventually escaped to the Mexican embassy in Lisbon and settled first in New York and later in Mexico, where she married the photographer Imre Weisz and had two sons. Carrington spent the rest of her life in Mexico City, moving in a circle of like-minded artists that included Remedios Varo and Alejandro Jodorowsky. Among Carrington's published works is a novel, *The Hearing Trumpet* (1976), and two collections of short stories. A group of stories she wrote for her children, collected as *The Milk of Dreams*, is published by The New York Review Children's Collection; her *Complete Stories* is published by Dorothy, a Publishing Project in the United States and by Silver Press in the United Kingdom.

MARINA WARNER's studies of religion, mythology, and fairy tales include *Alone of All Her Sex: The Myth and the Cult of the Virgin Mary*, *From the Beast to the Blonde*, and *Stranger Magic* (National Book Critics Circle Award for Literary Criticism; Truman Capote Prize). A Fellow of the British Academy, Warner is also a professor of English and creative writing at Birkbeck College, London. In 2015 she was given the Holberg Prize.

DOWN BELOW

LEONORA CARRINGTON

Introduction by
MARINA WARNER

NEW YORK REVIEW BOOKS

New York

THIS IS A NEW YORK REVIEW BOOK
PUBLISHED BY THE NEW YORK REVIEW OF BOOKS
435 Hudson Street, New York, NY 10014
www.nyrb.com

Library of Congress Cataloging-in-Publication Data
Names: Carrington, Leonora, 1917–2011, author.
Title: Down below / Leonora Carrington ; introduction by Marina Warner.
Description: New York : New York Review Books, 2017. | Series: NYRB
   Classics
Identifiers: LCCN 2016026859| ISBN 9781681370606 (softcover) | ISBN
   9781681370613 (epub)
Subjects: | BISAC: BIOGRAPHY & AUTOBIOGRAPHY / Artists,
   Architects, Photographers. | BIOGRAPHY & AUTOBIOGRAPHY /
   Personal Memoirs. | BIOGRAPHY & AUTOBIOGRAPHY / Women.
Classification: LCC PR6053.A6965 A6 2017 | DDC 823/.914—dc23
LC record available at https://lccn.loc.gov/2016026859

ISBN 978-1-68137-060-6
Available as an electronic book; ISBN 978-1-68137-061-3

Printed in the United States of America on acid-free paper.

10 9 8 7 6 5

CONTENTS

·

INTRODUCTION

THE YOUNG Leonora Carrington was determined to leap free of the dictates of her rich industrialist family: an early self-portrait shows a white horse (a perennial alter ego) leaping out of the window behind her, while a she-hyena (another familiar, another soul-sister), her udders leaking milk, comes docilely to the artist's hand. Edward James, the connoisseur and a patron of the surrealists, described Leonora, then a student artist, as "a ruthless English intellectual in revolt against all the hypocrisies of her homeland." In 1936, enrolled in the Ozenfant School of Fine Arts in London, she was already exploring her inner world, the "hypnagogic visions" that rose before her eyes when consciousness and the unconscious merge in the in-between of waking and sleeping, and she recognized, at the first International Surrealist Exhibition in London that year, an immediate kinship with the movement. Carrington's mother had given her a copy of Herbert Read's *Surrealism*. There she found, reproduced in the book, Max Ernst's assemblage-painting *Two Children Threatened by a Nightingale*, which struck her to the heart, she said. Several decades later, she would still remember how it felt: "a burning, inside; you know how when something really touches you, it feels like burning."

Max Ernst, born in 1891, has been somewhat eclipsed in the galaxy of artists of the period—Arshile Gorky, Meret Oppenheim, Lee Miller, Giorgio de Chirico—but at the time he was idolized: according to André Breton, the despotic arbiter of the surrealist pantheon, he was "the most magnificently haunted brain of our times." Ernst was Loplop, Prince of Birds, the surrealist movement's "Bird Superior," eclipsing all others in fame and prestige with his effortless gaiety and cruelty of invention, his unstinting ability to replenish the store of fantasies and improvise new media, new methods. He had realized the doctrine Breton had proclaimed in the first manifesto: *"N'importe quel merveilleux est beau, il n'y a meme que le merveilleux qui soit beau."* (Anything that is marvelous is beautiful, indeed only the marvelous is beautiful.)

When Leonora Carrington and Max Ernst met, she was nineteen years old and he was forty-six; she appeared to him as if directly summoned from the surrealist dream world, fulfilling every fantasy about the *femme-enfant*, the child-medium who excites the lover's imagination and moves him to fresher, stronger visions. Belief in the penetrating faculty of youth, in the young woman-child's closeness to mystery and sexuality, formed the crux of surrealist doctrine. In the fictional quest story *L'Amour fou*, published in 1937 (the same year Ernst met Carrington), Breton wrote a letter to his newborn daughter: "Let me believe that you will be ready then [on her sixteenth birthday] to embody the eternal power of woman, the only power before which I have ever bowed." To Breton the *femme-enfant* was a figure of salvation, because "in her and only her there seems to me to dwell, in a state of absolute transparency, the other prism of sight, which we stubbornly refuse to take into account, because it obeys laws which are very different, and which male despotism must prevent at all costs from being divulged." She was the "marvelously magnetic conductor," "the only one capable of retrieving that age of wildness." Ernst, in the autobiographical texts collected in *Beyond Painting*, recalled dreams teeming with such young women, and his frottages and collages conjure imaginary beings such as "the nymph Echo," "Perturbation, my sister," and Marceline-Marie, "the little girl who dreams of entering Carmel." In the preface he wrote to the short story "The House of Fear," Leonora was "*la mariée du vent*" incarnate, "the bride of the wind" of his desire, anticipated eleven years beforehand in the suite of prints *Histoire naturelle*.

Almost immediately, the couple left for Paris; she was to come back to England only once more, forty years later, for the funeral of her mother.

Soon after arriving in Paris, Leonora first exhibited her paintings in a show where the original sheets of Ernst's collage novel of 1934, *Une Semaine de bonté* (A Week of Kindness, or The Seven Capital Elements), were also displayed, showing a sweet-faced and imperturbable young protagonist endlessly subjected to floods and mayhem, fire and assault in a wickedly adroit parody of the penny-dreadful picture romance.

In this suite of images, and its earlier companions, *La Femme 100 têtes* (*The Hundred Headless Woman*) and *Rêve d'une petite fille que voulut entrer au carmel* (*A Little Girl Dreams of Taking the Veil*), Ernst mocks the rituals and ideals of his Catholic boyhood—Passion Week, the love language of the Song of Songs, martyrdom stories. Leonora had this in common with Ernst, that she had been brought up a Catholic and reveled in mischievous blasphemy to scandalize the *bien-pensants*.

In Paris, the couple rented an apartment, but extremely painful conflicts with Marie-Berthe Aurenche, to whom Ernst was still very much married and who was living in the city, as well as political quarrels within the fractious surrealist movement, drove them south. In the spring of 1938, they left Paris, and there began for Leonora a brief period of settled life in the village of Saint-Martin-d'Ardèche. She was sculpting, painting and writing—short fantastic fictions in an eccentric French. An artist's pamphlet, *La Maison de la peur* (*The House of Fear*), was the first to be published, in 1938, with its original spelling and grammar intact (Ernst in a foreword praised its "beautiful language, truthful and pure"), and signature collage illustrations by Ernst, composed from magazine engravings; a second collection, *La Dame ovale* (*The Oval Lady*), followed the year after. It included several of Carrington's most laconic and memorable tales—"The Debutante," "A Man in Love," "The Royal Summons," and "Uncle Sam Carrington"—again illustrated with fanciful, mock-solemn prints by Ernst.

These tales have Leonora's unique tone of voice, at once naive and perverse, comic and lethal, with the deadpan innocence of the masters of the macabre. The simplicity of her syntax and the cool sequential structure of the narrative heighten the delinquent pleasure of her voice: "She sucked, sucked for long minutes.... She threw back her head and crowed like a cock. Afterwards she hid the corpse in the drawer of a chest." The effect owes something to the restriction of using French, a language she had only studied with a French governess at home and in English convent schools. But unfamiliarity does not cramp her style; rather it sharpens the flavor of ingenuous knowingness that so enthralled the surrealists.

Ernst was an inspiring companion, she later acknowledged, with whom she discovered a new way of living; he could turn everything into play—cooking, keeping house, gardening. Memoirs of those days tell of excursions, general high spirits, practical jokes (there are some legendary surrealist exploits among them—Leonora cutting a guest's hair while he slept and sprinkling it into an omelette for flavor, or dyeing sago black with squid's ink and dishing it up with cracked ice and lemon as caviar for a collector paying a call). Although temperamentally she later resisted nostalgia and indeed reminiscing at all, she once let slip that this time just before war broke out was "an era of paradise."

The small stone Provençal farmhouse still stands on a hill above the deep valley of the Ardèche, east of the great gorges and natural arches carved by the spate of the river. The outside wall, facing the unpaved incline to the house, was sculpted by Ernst with towering fantastic creatures: a willowy young woman with a pigeon and a fish on her head holds a curled catlike totem in her left hand; beside her, a huge hieratic beaked monster raises his arms, while a smaller winged demon issues dancing from the wall beneath him. Behind the house a fragmentary carving of a horse lies on the broken wall, another white horse's head bares its teeth on the balustrade of the terrace. The beaked giant is easy to recognize as Ernst's alter ego, Loplop, Prince of Birds, and his partner as the mythologized figure of the surreal muse, incarnate in Leonora; the horse is a recurrent figure of release and power in her imagery. The inner walls of the courtyard are decorated in relief and painted, though—and this was more than twenty years ago—the pigments had faded and the concrete and plaster were eroding.

But Ernst's overweening ego (according to Peggy Guggenheim, he got cross when someone suggested Napoleon was the greater genius), combined with the coercive, cruel fantasies of surrealist sexuality, infuse many scenes that Leonora wrote and painted at the time with a degree of terror that rises above the usual range of the macabre tale. Célestin des Airlines-Drues, a character in the story "Pigeon, Fly!," wears the striped socks and cloak of feathers in which Leonora dressed Ernst in the portrait she painted of him in 1945. Here he is a frightening vampire, not an absurd or tender one. He asks the narrator to paint a picture of his dead wife—who turns out to be herself. Art becomes a death sentence, or at least a prophecy of a fatal conclusion.

Although they collaborated on the transformation of the house in Saint-Martin-d'Ardèche, Ernst did not encourage Leonora's art as much as he did her writing. It is easy to imagine, and perhaps not unjust, that he could inhabit her stories more fruitfully, and certainly his works of the period incorporate many Carrington motifs—horse-headed figures, journeys through craggy and forested landscapes out of the fairy-tale reading of her youth, mane-headed young women, emaciated ghouls.

The older artist, who had been married most of his adult life (Marie-Berthe was his second wife), also expected his *femme-enfant* to be a *femme de ménage*, and to provide for the stream of guests who flowed in from Paris and London and other points and stayed to talk, play, dress up, quarrel, tease one another, explore, and feast and drink—the house had its own vineyard. There is a series of photographs, taken by Lee Miller when she and Roland Penrose came to visit, which show Leonora in the kitchen, wearing a lace blouse and a long skirt that Leonor Fini, one of Ernst's "pets" —as Guggenheim later sharply put it—had bought in the Marché aux Puces in Paris. Later, on the same contact sheet, Ernst cradles his child bride, beaming to himself. What emerges from Leonora's steady look and the vigorous tilt of her head is that she was holding her own, but that it was hard, for she was being wrapped up in so much, posed in borrowed clothes, given a new language, cast to perform the role of the marvelous erotic and farouche child-wife to her much older lover. Fini painted her on several occasions at this time as a kind of Pre-Raphaelite Joan of Arc in black armor, engaged in enigmatic rites.

The charades, the fancy dress, the interplay of roles, both adoptive and prescribed, influence the fantastic metamorphoses in the stories: in an early tale, Arabelle Pégase, with her "dress made entirely of the heads of cats," represents another aspect of the immortal figure of Fear, whose house Leonora imagined herself to have entered. She's often Gothic in her humor, but the horror has its face towards real, endured experience. In this, she brings to mind Mary Shelley, who also fantasized improbable things and managed to survive Romanticism.

Carrington's own ambiguous homage to Ernst, published in New York in 1942 in the surrealist magazine *View*, evokes him in his persona of the Bird Superior, seizing Fear, of the many-furred hide and the hooves like white bats: "The Bird Superior ties fear to the flames of the fire by her tail and dips his feathered arms in the colour. Each feather immediately begins to paint a different image with the rapidity of a shriek...." This ferocious description of the making of art can be applied to Leonora herself: beneath the oneiric lyricism of her images, Fear lies pinioned, trying to break free.

In later years, Leonora would become angry when fans—like myself—showed intense curiosity about that early phase of her life. She once wrote me a furious letter—and letters from her were rare—because something I had written about her appeared with the photograph of Ernst leaning, blissed out, eyes closed, on her shoulder. Those old days were long ago for her, and she was not pleased when the intervening decades of work were not given their due. "A lot of people want to make me into gossip," she said, "and it's missing the point of anybody to make them into gossip."

When Leonora was born in 1917, the Carrington family was living in a huge Lancashire mansion called Crookhey Hall, and though they left it ten years later for a somewhat less imposing pile, it is Crookhey (Crackwood in her stories), with its gardeners and huntsmen and maids and "lavatory Gothic architecture," which provided the principal raw material for the many sites of captivity, suffocation, and punishment in her work, including the asylum in Spain and its grounds, as mapped in *Down Below*.

Her father, Harold, was a textile tycoon who sold the family concern, Carrington Cottons, to the large industrial company Courtaulds and became a principal shareholder of Imperial Chemicals Industries (ICI). His own father, a mill hand, had shown a flair for invention when he patented a new attachment for the looms; it led to the development of Viyella, a soft, blended cotton-and-wool twill every English child knows for its salutary properties of warmth, lightness, and durability.

The Carringtons were northerners, entrepreneurial, rough-and-ready. "You know what my father was most like?" Leonora once remarked. "A mafioso." By contrast, her maternal side, the Moorheads—Irish, Catholic—were easygoing and interested in magic and folklore. Her mother, Mairi, was the daughter of a country doctor from County Westmeath; she was "a complete mythologist," according to Leonora, and wove tall tales about the family, discovering connections far and wide, from the novelist Maria Edgeworth to Franz Joseph I of Austria. Leonora remembers a portrait of the emperor turning into an "ancestor." Mairi would read aloud the books of her favorite Irish writer, James Stephens, while Harold preferred the yarns of W. W. Jacobs—Gothic tales like "The Monkey's Paw." The tone of fey whimsy of Stephens's *The Crock of Gold* sometimes sounds in Leonora's writings; likewise, she turned to good account Jacobs's mix of macabre black magic and English heartiness. She also absorbed the English and Scottish nursery blend of nonsense, fabulism, comedy, and mysticism (Beatrix Potter, Lewis Carroll, Edward Lear, George MacDonald) and was told more ghost stories by her Irish nanny, Mary Kavanagh, the daughter of a prison warder. She had joined the family as a sewing maid at the age of sixteen or seventeen. (In one version of *Down Below*, Leonora describes her nanny as "my wet nurse, who had been with me till my twentieth year.") It was Nanny who was sent by her parents to fetch her back from Spain, and who arrived after a horrendous fortnight in the cabin of a warship (tradition has a submarine, but...) to find her darling girl in a madhouse. The plan was to go to South Africa to see out the war, but in the event, the rescue mission failed, as Leonora ran away to Portugal and then to the United States (but this is getting too far ahead of the story).

Leonora preferred to ignore the rich side of her background and recall instead that Moorhead is a Gypsy name. Nevertheless, according to the custom of the English upper classes, she was sent to boarding school, where she did not settle. With the help of the bishop of Lancaster, she was then moved to a second Catholic convent, St. Mary's, Ascot, in Berkshire, but the nuns were disturbed by her way of writing backwards with her left hand while writing forwards with her right (later in life, she also painted with both hands at the same time). When this school also gave up on her, Leonora went to Italy to be "finished" at Miss Penrose's Academy in the Piazza Donatello, Florence. There she began looking at the artists who were to shape her vision, inspiring her intimacy with the supernatural, her sequential storytelling, her use of tempera, and her love of cinnabar, vermilion, umber, earth colors, and gold: the Tuscan masters of the trecento and quattrocento (Sassetta, Francesco di Giorgio, Giovanni di Paolo, Fra Angelico).

She came back to England determined to be an artist, but her father considered painting "horrible and idiotic": "You didn't do art," she recalled him saying. "If you did, you were either poor or homosexual, which were more or less the same sort of crime." She was obliged to "come out," that is, "do the season," which was another custom of her class; her parents gave her a showy dance at the Ritz—there is a splendid official photograph of her in white satin and lilies, being presented at court in the last year of George V's reign. She was destined for a life of prosperous tedium.

These experiences return, nightmarishly, in her stories, especially the one called "The Debutante." But in the teeth of her father's opposition, she insisted on returning to art school, and enrolled at Ozenfant's.

The spell in the "paradise" of Provence was to be cut short: what Leonora called "Max's genital responsibilities" took him to Paris; soon afterwards, war broke out, the Germans invaded, and France collapsed. She captures these times of loneliness and struggle in the stories she was writing at the time, which include the novella *Little Francis*, and they give strong warning signs of the danger she was in and the role of her irrepressible creativity in withstanding the worst. She had been curious to enter the house of fear, but she had not expected that its doors would shut on her so ineluctably.

During the winter when Ernst left her in Saint-Martin-d'Ardèche while he sorted out his marriage, Leonora was taken in by Alphonsine, the local café's proprietress: "I didn't think he'd ever come back, I didn't know where I was going. I was like a monster. At least I felt like some sort of performing animal, a bear with a ring in its nose. I was *l'Anglaise*, and the café, which never had anyone in it, became crowded." She first transforms this experience in *Little Francis*, adding the story about a woman who, seduced by a bullfighter who's a nose fetishist, embellishes her nose with tattoos and a ring. She said of such an experience, "I think it's death practice."

In 1939, after the French declared war on Germany, Ernst was arrested as an enemy alien and sent to a camp at Largentière. Leonora followed him there, supplying him with paints and other materials, and lobbying influential friends in Paris for his release. She—and other contacts—succeeded, and Ernst returned to Saint-Martin-d'Ardèche. Early the following year, after the Germans crossed the Maginot Line, he was arrested again—he was a known undesirable to the invaders; his painting *La Belle Jardinière* had toured the country in the Nazis' show of "degenerate art." This time, he was imprisoned farther away, at Les Milles near Aix, with hundreds of other "aliens" (including Hans Bellmer, who painted his portrait there). Leonora again traveled to Paris to sue for his freedom, but she now found closed doors everywhere. She returned to Saint-Martin-d'Ardèche and, unable to do more to rescue him and aware of the advancing German army, her friends scattering in panic, she suffered an attack of deep despair, leading to the symptoms she describes so harrowingly in *Down Below.*

Eventually she was helped to leave France by an English friend, who took her across the Pyrenees; she handed over the house and all its contents into the safekeeping of one of the villagers before leaving (when Ernst, before his final escape from France, found his way back to Saint-Martin-d'Ardèche, he was denied access to the property). In Madrid, after erratic and highly disturbed episodes, Leonora was hospitalized, then transferred to the asylum of Dr. Morales in Santander and given a course of drug therapy with Cardiazol, which induced epileptic fits of appalling severity.

Her descent into madness consecrated her as a surrealist heroine, regardless of the cost of her sufferings. The "*dérèglement de tous les sens*" (the derangement of all the senses) sought by Rimbaud did not bring about the "breakthrough" to enlightenment the surrealist *merveilleux* promised, and *Down Below* reflects this ambivalence. "After the experience of *Down Below*, I changed," Leonora remembered. "Dramatically. It was very much like having been dead. It was very clear, I was possessed. I'd suffered so much when Max was taken away to the camp, I entered a catatonic state, and I was no longer suffering in an ordinary human dimension. I was in another place, it was something quite different. Quite different."

Magouche Fielding, who in the forties was married to Arshile Gorky in New York, once commented drily, "Surrealism wasn't good for your health. I don't think anyone would take it as a cure. It was like filleting fish, taking out the backbone of quite ordinary people. Max Ernst, now, was as strong as an ox." Leonora often referred to the "terror" she felt and continued to feel, and although she fortunately never had to contend again with anything like the prolonged bout of insanity described in *Down Below*, she feared a recurrence.

In the postscript appended here to the 1943 version

of *Down Below*, she tells the story of her escape from
Spain, as she remembered it in 1987. She had married
Renato Leduc, a Mexican diplomat whom she had
first met with Picasso in Paris—Leduc was a bullfighting crony of the artist's. Meanwhile, Guggenheim was coming to the rescue of many of the
surrealists, including Ernst, with whom she fell painfully in love and whom she took to Lisbon, along with
her former husband Laurence Vail, his wife the writer
Kay Boyle, and half a dozen children from various
marriages, in order to take the Clipper, the first of the
transatlantic passenger planes. Lou Straus, Ernst's
first wife and the mother of his only child, Jimmy, did
not escape; she was deported from a Paris detention
camp to Auschwitz on one of the last trains, on June
30, 1944.

In Lisbon, Max and Leonora met again; she recalled
that after all her recent ordeals, she found herself free
at last from the spell Loplop had once exercised over
her. Guggenheim observes, in her memoirs: "God
knows how she ever got out of the place [the asylum]
but after she did, she met the Mexican in Lisbon and
he looked after her. He was like a father to her. Max
was always like a baby and couldn't be anyone's father.
I think she felt she needed a father more than anything else, so as to give her some stability and prevent
her from going mad again."

Leonora always spoke warmly of Guggenheim, saying that she was remarkably generous; although Ernst's
clear attachment to Leonora caused her much pain,
Guggenheim offered to pay for Leonora's passage to

New York on the plane with them. Leonora refused, and when the Guggenheim household left, on July 13, 1941, "we passed over the American boat that was carrying Leonora and her husband to New York."

In New York, their interwoven lives continued: the surrealists in exile produced papers, journals (*VVV* and *View*), and, with Guggenheim's help, exhibitions. Leonora's art was changing. She had seen Bosch's paintings in the Prado in Madrid and in Lisbon and their influence was profound, as anyone who has encountered her work knows. Bosch paints "the imaginal space we all live in," which she felt begins to take over more strongly as one grows older. During the war she developed the intricately visionary style of her mature art, peopling her panels with dreamscapes, imaginary beings, smoking volcanoes, ice floes. The portrait of Ernst she made at this time seems to offer a reply to Ernst's grandiloquent 1940 work *The Robing of the Bride*; the red feathers of his mermaid's-tail cloak echo the scarlet feathered robe of the bride herself. In the Carrington image, the white unicorn, her animal familiar, appears twice—frozen in the icy landscape and again trapped in the glass lantern Ernst holds in his hand. He gave her a portrait in turn, *Leonora in the Morning Light*, showing her rising out of a jungle, parting its tentacular growth; during this period he also painted *Spanish Physician*, showing a Leonora-like young woman screaming as she runs from a monstrous minotaur-like beast.

In the eighties, when she was living in New York, Leonora resisted inquiry into the interactions between the two artists, their imagery and symbols; it was eerie, when I visited the Metropolitan Museum with her in 1987, to pass by, without any comment from her, the painting entitled *Napoleon in the Desert* (1940), in which Ernst portrays himself with a horse's head on a rocky outcrop, while beside him, a beautiful bride figure holds herself at a distance, unmoved by his presence.

Down Below gives an unsparing account of the experience of being insane. As an act of truth-telling memory, it derives its power from this antinomy at its heart, that it is a narrative, apparently rationally composed and accurately recalled, about hair-raisingly unhinged behavior and cruel, scientific therapies that induced states of personal annihilation. Breton encouraged Leonora to write it; from his point of view, the English artist, wild muse, *femme-enfant*, had realized one of the most desirable ambitions of surrealism, the katabasis of the modern age, the voyage to the other side of reason. In the preface to Ernst's *Hundred Headless Woman*, Breton had spoken of "our will to absolute disorientation." She was Nadja *retrouvée*, the heroine of Breton's text returned from the lower depths, an instrument of *l'amour fou* and its victim. She had truly experienced the derangement Breton and Paul Éluard had only been able to simulate in *L'Immaculée Conception* in 1930, though their impersonation of insanity later won Jacques Lacan's applause.

Down Below was composed with hindsight, and so it differs from the many pieces of fiction Leonora was writing earlier, as events unfolded. *Down Below* is factual in approach and style, written in the form of a diary, and offers a unique act of remembrance, almost incredibly circumstantial; it combines lucid retrieval and hallucinatory madness in a record that is the persevering work of an artist and a writer at the same time as the haphazard record of a patient. The title echoes mythological and literary descents into hell (Dostoyevsky and Rimbaud, as well as classic precursors familiar to her after her religious upbringing), but at the same time the depths—"down below"—are represented as an actual safe place, a sanctuary within the grounds of the asylum, where the writer dreams of going because there the horrific treatments (the agonizing injections with Cardiazol) will stop. As a testament to madness, it is split between visionary illumination and profound psychological distress. It is a classic of the genre, ranking among the most lacerating messages from the other side—Carl Jung's *The Red Book: Liber Novus*, Daniel Paul Schreber's *Memoirs of My Nervous Illness*, and Henri Michaux's *Miserable Miracle*.

Like several of Leonora Carrington's writings, *Down Below* has had a complicated history of migrations and variants: she first wrote a short version in English in 1942 in New York and showed it to Janet Flanner, who was then working as a publisher but, surprisingly, wasn't interested. This draft was lost when Leonora left for Mexico (she was always marvelously unworldly about her property, intellectual and other); however, Pierre Mabille, a friend of hers in the fugitive community there, a surgeon and an intimate of the surrealist circle in France, urged her to reconstruct it. The "you" in the opening paragraph is Mabille, and in August 1943, she began to relate this version in the abandoned Russian embassy in Mexico City, where she, Mabille, and other refugees were squatting, on the third anniversary of the events she recalls. Leonora then talked it through in French to Jeanne Megnen, Mabille's wife, who established the first published version in French. This was then translated back into English by Victor Llona for the surrealist journal *VVV*, edited in New York by David Hare and, for a period, Marcel Duchamp. *Down Below* came out in the February 1944 issue, soon after the short story "The Seventh Horse"; nearly two years later, Henri Parisot, the publisher-editor who had brought out Leonora's stories before the war, was able to publish it in France, where it appeared in the series L'Age d'Or immediately after the war ended.

This journey to and fro, between oral and written versions, and French and English translations, accounts in part for the major difference in tone between *Down Below* and Leonora's other writings. As a testament to the horrors of psychosis, as evidence of medical treatment and convulsive drug therapy, *Down Below* ranks beside autobiographical fiction of such desperate conditions, as captured in Antonia White's *The Sugar House*, Sylvia Plath's *The Bell Jar*, and Janet Frame's *Faces in the Water*. It often strikes occult resemblances with Leonora's novella *The Stone Door*, but it has only moments of her distinctive drollness. On a literary level, however, *Down Below* belongs more closely to the genre of autobiographical record advocated by Breton and practiced by him in both *Nadja* and *L'Amour fou*; tracing off daily experience, the writer-seeker uncovers marvelous patternings brought about by *le hasard objectif* (objective chance) and reaches illumination. In its pitilessness, too (though it can provoke pity, *Down Below* shows very little to herself or towards others), the work reflects surrealism's cult of madness, especially female madness, as another conductor to the invisible world.

Like Gisèle Prassinos, the child poet whom the surrealists idolized, or Violette Nozière and Lizzie Borden, who as delinquents—as murderers—likewise inspired their admiration, or the convulsionary women of St. Médard in the eighteenth century and the hysterics whom Jean-Martin Charcot had photographed in attitudes of despair and desire, Leonora in her crazed state met surrealist ideals of escape from bourgeois convention. Her torments confirmed her status as a kind of hierodule, a holy and erotic nymph who uniquely knew by instinct certain delinquent mysteries that the older men of surrealism felt they could not reach without her help.

"The task of the right eye is to peer into the telescope, while the left eye peers into the microscope," she declares in *Down Below*. Her experiences of relations between herself and the world—animals, rocks, other people—share distortions of perspective along these lines, microcosms magnified, details projected into far horizons, occult meanings encrypted in random patterns. Breton elevated the idea of random chance into a principle of art, and the narrator here remembers the coherence she found in scattered circumstances, the conspiracies she detected, and the bewildering number of people she met, who make appearances like so many phantoms of a nightmare from which you cannot wake. As in case studies such as Victor Tausk's "On the Origin of the 'Influencing Machine' in Schizophrenia," Leonora felt that the doctors and others around her—the sinister Van Ghent, Mr. Gilliland (the agent of her father's company ICI), the Moraleses (father and son—she draws a fine portrait of one of them), the nurses Piadosa and Frau Asegurado, José, Alberto—were exercising dark powers over the world as well as punishing her for her unique grasp of their nefarious plans. *Down Below* catches very powerfully her own utter disempowerment and at the same time her conviction—insane, crazy—that only she could see what was truly happening. After arriving in Madrid, she describes how she went to the hotel room of her friend Catherine, who had helped her cross the Pyrenees: "I begged her to look at my face; I said to her: 'Don't you see that it is the exact representation of the world?'"

As a narrator, the author/memoirist swerves between viewpoints: she deploys huge narratives from afar—her figures can be tiny—and then works in embroiderer's detail, close-up, introducing smaller creatures into the fabric of the larger ones. The map of the asylum at Santander, where the longed-for haven of "Down Below" appears in a flaming halo, includes a minute drawing near the "apple trees" of a horse buckled and upturned, as if felled by a cannon shot: a self-portrait of herself undergoing the violent treatments she describes?

It is significant that Carrington often painted faces with unmatched eyes, like *The Ancestor* (1968), or the piebald dogs with a patch round one eye who appear in *Bird Seizes Jewel* (1969), as well as several more paintings of the late eighties. Her disoriented consciousness in *Down Below* never returned destructively again (though, as I say, she lived in fear that it might), but she continued to inhabit, for oneiric and expressive purposes, a shifting angle of view and doubled vision both inside and outside the narrating self. Or perhaps I should say, selves? For she was convinced of the plurality of the self and believed in the Buddhist doctrine of metempsychosis (the migration of the soul into other bodies after death), and felt sympathy with all matter, without hierarchy. In *Down Below*, she describes how she sought "through gentleness an understanding between the mountain, my body, and my mind," how she talked to animals "through the skin, by means of a sort of 'touch' language. . . . I could draw near animals where other human beings put them to precipitate flight."

Since her childhood, Leonora Carrington had been a questor, looking for a scripture to match her belief in the metaphysical dimensions of existence. She continued to be fascinated by divination, magic, horoscopes, and sorcery of all kinds. Although her endless metaphysical search was undertaken in earnest, it was never carried out with solemnity. At one time she was deeply involved in alchemy, but she brought to its tabulations the light fantastic touch of a fairy-tale wizard rather than the bombast of a guru. Although she believed that there is something to find—the philosopher's stone—she did not believe that she had special powers to reach it or that she ever would. True to character, she could see the comic side of her lifelong search, secular and religious, while keenly continuing to pursue it. Her encounter with the spiritual leader and teacher G. I. Gurdjieff inspired her sparkling satire of Lightsome Hall and its guru, Dr. Gambit, in *The Hearing Trumpet*, a comic tour de force, which was written in the fifties and published in English in 1976. For many years she was a disciple of Tibetan Buddhism, making several retreats, both in the Tibetan monastery in Scotland, where she first went with Anne Fremantle in the early seventies (the last time she visited Britain), and in upstate New York during the eighties. Drawing on a range of mystical symbols with eclectic high spirits, she offers images and enigmas that resemble koans, the Zen puzzles that, having no solution in the realm of reason, produce the release of laughter.

Leaving the personal body, abandoning fixed identity, and descending to the depths of anguish, evoked in *Down Below* as terrifying, are shamanic states that hold compulsive fascination for the uninitiated; the visions in *Down Below* have set Leonora Carrington in a constellation of illuminati alongside William Blake, Rimbaud, Aldous Huxley, Bob Dylan, and, most recently, Patti Smith.

In 1942, Leonora left New York for Mexico, where the socialist government, in a gesture of visionary generosity, had offered citizenship to any refugees from Fascism. Many surrealists responded and gathered in Mexico City: these refugees included the poet Benjamin Péret and his wife, the artist Remedios Varo, who were to become intimate friends of Leonora's. Breton had visited Mexico in 1938 and declared, on his return, *"La Mexique est surréaliste en elle-même"* (Mexico is surrealist in itself), with its mythic past, cult of the dead, art of the fantastic, and astonishing landscapes. Leonora's marriage of convenience to Renato Leduc, who was working as a bullfighting reporter, was amicable—"a nice man," she once said, "neglectful, but nice"—and they soon divorced; she married Imre Weisz, known as "Cziki," a newspaper photographer who had left Hungary with Robert Capa, scraped by with him in Paris, and then left to take part in the Spanish Civil War. On their return, as Capa became more and more successful, Weisz began running his studio in Paris; the Occupation swept him up, along with so many others, and he too took refuge in Mexico City.

With Cziki, Leonora had two sons, Gabriel (b. 1946) and Pablo (b. 1948): the experience of motherhood led her into new depths of knowledge, and far from depleting her creative powers, strengthened them: "I believe that for female animals the act of love, which is followed by the great drama of the birth of a new animal, pushes us into the biological underworld, very deeply...." Bringing up her sons affirmed for her all over again the high value of the creaturely: she painted the ecstatic procession of *L'Amor che move il sole e l'altre stelle* in the week of her first child's birth.

She was painting for their livelihood, including, she admitted to me cheerfully, fakes. A commission for a painting that was to appear in a film led to a famished dream of abundance: "The bald-headed girl in the red dress combines female charm and the delights of the table—you will notice that she is engaged in making an unctuous broth of (let us say) lobsters, mushrooms, fat turtle, spring chicken, ripe tomatoes, Gorgonzola cheese, milk chocolate, onions, and tinned peaches. The mixture of these ingredients has overflowed and taken on a greenish and sickly hue to the fevered vision of Saint Anthony, whose daily meal consists of withered grass and tepid water with an occasional locust by way of an orgy."

At the time, Leonora was living mainly on ice cream, "which was the cheapest thing you could get," so the saint's imaginings have a certain urgency (those tinned peaches tell of scarcity very clearly). She was paid $200 for the picture, which was "a considerable fortune at that time."

In Mexico, she encountered a culture in which the beliefs of the Indians merged with the imported Catholicism of the missionaries and the conquistadores;

in the vigorous spirit of this Mexican syncretism, the artist wanted to communicate her inner visions, and a luxuriant variety of religious symbols bloom in her paintings of this period. "All religions are real," Leonora once commented. "But you have to go through your own channels—you might meet the Egyptians, you might meet with the Voodoos, but in order to keep some kind of equilibrium it has to feel authentic to you."

Remedios Varo was her co-conspirator during this fertile time; the two women were symbiotic in their restless inventiveness and explorings; in a feminist spirit of inquiry, they wrote fables and plays together and made paintings of dream states and mythic journeys. Varo's intricate, extraordinary allegories of this period reveal a rare sympathy and joie de vivre in the friendship. They managed to combine seriousness with high spirits as they touched off inspiration in each other. Varo's unexpected death at the age of fifty-four in 1963 was the hardest loss Leonora suffered, she told me, and she always spoke of it with intense distress.

Internal division, mystical affinities, shape-shifting can be fertile; the way through the stone door needs many vehicles, plural morphologies, and metamorphoses, not totemic integrity. So although her imagination is sui generis, original, and personal, Leonora repudiated the notion of a unified, artistic personality that such praise assumes as its premise. This is the paradox of her personality as well as her oeuvre. In her very denials of so many of the foundations of Western ideas about sanity and the unified self, she comes near to fulfilling deeply shared Western longings for Original Genius. Above all, she has become a beacon for women artists and writers, a model of self-willed dedication to her gifts, in the face of all the obstacles society set in her way. Carrington's young she-beasts literally hold their heads high in *Night Nursery Everything* (1947), *Baby Giant* (1947), the sculpture *Cat Woman* (also known as *La Grande Dame*, 1951), and *And Then We Saw the Daughter of the Minotaur* (1953).

Widely read in alchemical writings, analyzed by followers of Jung, and loyal to a fierce and personal brand of idealism, which the art historian Janice Helland has called "esoteric feminism," Leonora never altogether shed her wonderful spirit of irreverent mischief. Her great friend and collector Edward James wrote above her door in Mexico, "This is the house of the Sphinx." A sphinx, yes, but a sphinx who sets riddles not to confound or destroy but to provoke laughter and open doors in the chambers of the mind, where love and fear and the other passions have their seat. She has said, "I try to empty myself of images which have made me blind." In many ways she was breaking spells that blind others' sight too. "Ironic sorcery": Carlos Fuentes's fine phrase captures well the sustained mixed tone of her vision—and her voice.

Leonora would remain in Mexico until her death in 2011, in her house in Cuernavaca, with only occasional longish periods in New York (she would never fly but always took the bus). She had left behind the confusions of her English and French lives. *Penelope*

(1946), a stage play, ends on a new note of savage optimism, with the heroine's escape on her horse, Tartar, and the suicide of her repressive father. Leonora once told me that her favorite story from the Bible was Jacob wrestling with the angel. "We have to hang on," she said. "Even if the angel cries, 'Let me go, let me go.' We don't listen. No. We have to hang on." There's a ladder there, in the background of the biblical account, waiting to be climbed to heaven, but for the moment the here and now on the ground demands struggle. Through the journeys and the sufferings that her writing transcribes and transforms, Leonora Carrington held on, sometimes laughing wickedly, sometimes fighting mad.

—MARINA WARNER
Kentish Town, London, 2017

Notes and Further Reading

All quotations when not otherwise attributed are from conversations with Leonora held from 1986 to 1988, when she was living in New York. I was writing a filmscript inspired by her life and work for the director Gina Newson, and though nothing came of the project, those days I spent with Leonora, walking through the streets of Manhattan and all around Central Park, and the hours we spent talking, count among the most inspiring experiences of my life. Some of this material, reprised here, appeared in the introductions to two volumes of her collected stories, *The House of Fear* and *The Seventh Horse*.

I should like to express my thanks to the late David Cardiff, my contemporary at university who introduced me to Leonora's paintings through the collection of his father, Maurice Cardiff, who had been the British consul in Mexico City and, along with his wife (also called Leonora), was a close friend and associate. I also owe thanks to many scholars, especially Whitney Chadwick.

Aberth, Susan L. *Leonora Carrington: Surrealism, Alchemy and Art.* Burlington, VT: Lund Humphries, 2010.

American Federation of Arts et al. *The Temptation of St. Anthony: An Exhibition of Eleven Paintings by Noted American and European Artists.* Washington, DC: American Federation of Arts, 1947.

Arcq, Teresa, Joanna Moorhead, and Stefan von Raaij, eds. *Surreal Friends. Leonora Carrington, Remedios Varo and Kati Horna.* Burlington, VT: Lund Humphries, 2010.

Breton, André, ed. *Anthologie de l'humour noir.* Paris: Éditions du Sagittaire, 1950.

Breton, André, and Marcel Duchamp, eds. *First Papers of Surrealism.* New York: Coordinating Council of French Relief Societies, 1942.

Carrington, Leonora. *The House of Fear: Notes from Down Below.* Translated by Kathrine Talbot with Marina Warner. New York: E. P. Dutton, 1988; London: Virago, 1988.

———. *The Seventh Horse and Other Tales.* Translated by

Kathrine Talbot with Marina Warner. New York: E. P. Dutton, 1988; London: Virago, 1989.

Carrington, Leonora, and Juan García Ponce. *Leonora Carrington*. Mexico: Ediciones Era, 1974.

Carrington, Leonora, and Annie Le Brun et al. *Leonora Carrington. La mariée du vent*. Paris: Gallimard, Maison de l'Amérique latine, 2008.

Carrington, Leonora, and Mexican Museum. *Leonora Carrington—the Mexican Years: 1943–1985*. San Francisco: Mexican Museum, 1991.

Chadwick, Whitney. *Women Artists and the Surrealist Movement*. London: Thames & Hudson, 1986.

Ernst, Jimmy. *A Not-So-Still Life: A Memoir*. New York: St. Martin's/Marek, 1984.

Guggenheim, Peggy. *Out of This Century: Confessions of an Art Addict*. New York: Universe Books, 1979.

Helland, Janice. *Daughter of the Minotaur: Leonora Carrington and the Surrealist Image*. Victoria, BC: University of Victoria, 1984.

———. "Surrealism and Esoteric Feminism in the Art of Leonora Carrington." *Canadian Art Review* 16, No. 1 (1989), 53–104.

James, Edward. *Leonora Carrington: A Retrospective Exhibition*. New York: Center for Inter-American Relations, 1975.

Kaplan, Janet A. *Unexpected Journeys: The Art and Life of Remedios Varo*. London: Virago, 1988.

Noël, Bernard. *La Planète affolée: Surréalisme, dispersion et influences 1938–1941*. Paris: Musée de Marseille, 1986.

Orenstein, Gloria Feman. "Hermeticism and Surrealism in the Visual Works of Leonora Carrington as a Model for Latin American Symbology." *Proceedings of the 10th Congress of the International Comparative Literature Association*. Edited by Anna Balakian. New York: New York University, 1985.

Poniatowska, Elena. *Leonora*. Translated by Amanda Hopkinson. London: Serpent's Tail, 2014.

Rudenstine, Angelica Zander. *The Peggy Guggenheim Collection, Venice*. New York: Harry Abrams, 1985.

Suleiman, Susan Rubin. *Subversive Intent: Gender, Politics, and the Avant-Garde.* Cambridge, MA: Harvard University Press, 1990.

Walsh, Joanna. "'I have no delusions. I am playing'—Leonora Carrington's Madness and Art." *Verso* (blog). Posted October 9, 2015 at www.versobooks.com/blogs/2275-i-have-no-delusions-i-am-playing-leonora-carrington-s-madness-and-art and accessed February 10, 2017.

Warner, Marina. "Leonora Carrington: Brewster Gallery, New York." *Burlington Magazine* 130 (October 1988), 796–97.

———. "The Spirit Bestiary of Leonora Carrington." In *Leonora Carrington: Paintings, Drawings and Sculptures, 1940–1990.* Edited by Andrea Schlieker. London: Serpentine Gallery, 1991.

DOWN BELOW

Lee Miller, portrait of Leonora Carrington, Saint-Martin-d'Ardèche, 1939.
Photograph © 2017 by Lee Miller Archives, England.

Exactly three years ago, I was interned in Dr. Morales's sanatorium in Santander, Spain, Dr. Pardo, of Madrid, and the British Consul having pronounced me incurably insane. Since I fortuitously met you, whom I consider the most clear-sighted of all, I began gathering a week ago the threads which might have led me across the initial border of Knowledge. I must live through that experience all over again, because, by doing so, I believe that I may be of use to you, just as I believe that you will be of help in my journey beyond that frontier by keeping me lucid and by enabling me to put on and to take off at will the mask which will be my shield against the hostility of Conformism.

Before taking up the actual facts of my experience, I want to say that the sentence passed on me by society at that particular time was probably, surely even, a god-send, for I was not aware of the importance of health, I mean of the absolute necessity of having a healthy body to avoid disaster in the liberation of the mind. More important yet, the necessity that others be with me that we may feed each other with our knowledge and thus constitute the Whole.

I was not sufficiently conscious at the time of your philosophy to understand. *The time had not come for me to understand.* What I am going to endeavor to express here with the utmost fidelity was but an embryo of knowledge.

I begin therefore with the moment when Max was taken away to a concentration camp for the second time, under the escort of a gendarme who carried a rifle (May 1940). I was living in Saint-Martin-d'Ardèche. I wept for several hours, down in the village; then I went up again to my house where, for twenty-four hours, I indulged in voluntary vomitings induced by drinking orange blossom water and interrupted by a short nap. I hoped that my sorrow would be diminished by these spasms, which tore at my stomach like earthquakes. I know now that this was but one of the aspects of those vomitings: I had realised the injustice of society, I wanted first of all to cleanse myself, then go beyond its brutal ineptitude. My stomach was the seat of that society, but also the place in which I was united with all the elements of the earth. It was the *mirror* of the earth, the reflection of which is just as real as the person reflected. That mirror—my stomach—had to be rid of the thick layers of filth (the accepted formulas) in order properly, clearly, and faithfully to reflect the earth; and when I say "the earth," I mean of course all the earths, stars, suns in the sky and on the earth, as well as all the stars, suns, and earths of the microbes' solar system.

For three weeks I ate very sparingly, carefully eschewing meat, and drank wine and alcohol, feeding on potatoes and salad, at the rate perhaps of two potatoes a day. My impression is that I slept pretty well. I worked at my vines, astonishing the peasants by my strength. Saint John's Day was near at hand, the vines were beginning to blossom, they had to be sprayed often with sulphur. I also worked at my potatoes, and the more I sweated, the better I liked it, because this meant that I was getting purified. I took sunbaths, and my physical strength was such as I have never known before or afterwards.

Various events were taking place in the outside world: the collapse of Belgium, the entry of the Germans in France. All of this interested me very little and I had no fear whatsoever within me. The village was thronged with Belgians, and some soldiers who had entered my home accused me of being a spy and threatened to shoot me on the spot because someone had been looking for snails at night, with a lantern, near my house. Their threats impressed me very little indeed, for I knew that I was not destined to die.

After three solitary weeks, Catherine, an Englishwoman, a very old friend of mine, arrived, fleeing from Paris with Michel Lucas, a Hungarian. A week went by and I believe they noticed nothing abnormal in me. One day, however, Catherine, who had been for a long time under the care of psychoanalysts, persuaded me that my attitude betrayed an unconscious desire to get rid for the second time of my father: Max, whom I had to eliminate if I wanted to live. She begged me to cease punishing myself and to look for another lover. I think she was mistaken when she said I was torturing myself. I think that she interpreted me fragmentarily, which is worse than not to interpret at all. However, by doing so she restored me to sexual desire. I tried frantically to seduce two young men, but without success. They would have none of me. And I had to remain sadly chaste.

The Germans were approaching rapidly; Catherine frightened me and begged me to leave with her, saying that if I refused to do so, she too would remain. I accepted. I accepted above all because, in my evolution, Spain represented for me Discovery. I accepted because I expected to get a visa put in Max's passport in Madrid. I still felt bound to Max. This document, which bore his image, became an entity, as if I was taking Max with me. I accepted, somewhat touched by Catherine's arguments, which were distilling into me, hour after hour, a growing fear. For Catherine, the Germans meant rape. I was not afraid of that, I attached no importance to it. What caused panic to rise within me was the thought of robots, of thought-less, fleshless beings.

Michel and I decided to go to Bourg-Saint-Andéol to secure a travelling permit. The gendarmes, totally indifferent and uninterested, kept on smoking ciga-rettes and refused to give us the bit of paper, barricad-ing themselves behind phrases like "we can't do anything about it." We were unable to leave, yet I knew that we would leave the following day. We went to the notary, where I made over to the proprietor of the Motel des Touristes of Saint-Martin my house and all my goods. I returned home and spent the whole night carefully sorting the things I intended taking along with me. All of them got into a suitcase which bore, beneath my name, a small brass plate set into the leather, on which was written the word REV-ELATION.

In Saint-Martin next morning, the schoolmistress gave me papers stamped by the town hall, which made it possible for us to depart. Catherine got the car ready. All my willpower strained towards that depar-ture. I hurried my friends. I pushed Catherine toward the car; she took the wheel; I sat between her and Mi-chel. The car started. I was confident in the success of the journey, but terribly anguished, fearing difficulties which I thought inevitable. We were riding normally when, twenty kilometres beyond Saint-Martin, the car stopped; the brakes had jammed. I heard Cathe-rine say: "The brakes have jammed." "Jammed!" I, too, was jammed within, by forces foreign to my conscious will, which were also paralyzing the mechanism of the car. This was the first stage of my identification with the external world. I was the car. The car had jammed on account of me, because I, too, was jammed between Saint-Martin and Spain. I was horrified by my own power. At that time, I was still limited to my own so-lar system, and was not aware of other people's sys-tems, the importance of which I realise now.

We had driven all night long. I would see before

me, on the road, trucks with legs and arms dangling behind them, but being unsure of myself, I would say shyly: "There are trucks ahead of us," just to find out what the answer would be. When they said: "The road is wide, we'll manage to bypass them," I felt reassured; but I did not know whether or not they saw what was carried in those trucks, greatly fearing I would arouse their suspicions and becoming prey to shame, which paralysed me. The road was lined with rows of coffins, but I could find no pretext to draw their attention to this embarrassing subject. They obviously were people who had been killed by the Germans. I was very frightened: *it all stank of death*. I learned later that there was a huge military cemetery in Perpignan.

In Perpignan, at seven in the morning, there were no rooms in the hotels. My friends had left me in a cafe; from then on, I had no rest: I was convinced I was responsible for my friends. I believed that it was useless to call on the higher authorities if we wanted to cross the border, and I sought instead the advice of boot-blacks, cafe waiters, and passersby who I thought were vested with tremendous power.

We were to meet, at a point two kilometres distant from Andorra, with two Andorrans who were supposed to get us across the border in exchange for the gift of our car. Catherine and Michel told me very seriously that I had better refrain from talking. I agreed and dived into a voluntary coma.

When we reached Andorra, I could not walk straight. I walked like a crab; I had lost control over my motions: an attempt at climbing stairs would again bring about a "jam."

In Andorra—a deserted and godforsaken country—we were the first refugees to be received in the Hôtel de France by a little maidservant who bore the entire responsibility for that strangely empty establishment.

My first steps in Andorra meant to me what the first steps on a tightrope must mean to an acrobat. At night, my exasperated nerves imitated the noise of the river, which flowed tirelessly over some rocks: hypnotizing, monotonous.

By day, we tried to walk about on the mountainside, but no sooner would I attempt to ascend the slightest slope than I would jam like Catherine's Fiat, and be compelled to climb down again. My anguish jammed me completely.

I realized that my anguish—my mind, if you prefer—was painfully trying to unite itself with my body; my mind could no longer manifest itself without producing an immediate effect on my body—on matter. Later it would exercise itself upon other objects. I was trying to understand this vertigo of mine: that my body no longer obeyed the formulas established in my mind, the formulas of old, limited Reason; that my will no longer meshed with my faculties of movement, and since my will no longer possessed any power, it was necessary first to liquidate my paralyzing anguish, then to seek an accord between the mountain, my mind, and my body. In order to be able to move around in this new world, I had recourse to my heritage of British diplomacy and set aside the strength of my will, seeking through gentleness an understanding between the mountain, my body, and my mind.

One day I went to the mountain alone. At first I could not climb; I lay flat on my face on the slope with the sensation that I was being completely absorbed by the earth. When I took the first steps up the slope, I had the physical sensation of walking with tremendous effort in some matter as thick as mud. Gradually, however, perceptibly and visibly, it all became easier, and in a few days I was able to negotiate jumps. I could climb vertical walls as easily as any goat. I very seldom got hurt, and I realised the possibility of a very subtle understanding which I had not perceived before. Finally, I managed to take no false steps and to wander around quite easily among the rocks.

It is obvious that, for the ordinary citizen, this must have taken on a strange and crazy aspect: a well-brought-up young Englishwoman jumping from one rock to another, amusing herself in so irrational a manner: this was wont to raise immediate suspicions as to my mental balance. I gave little thought to the effect my experiments might have on the humans by whom I was surrounded, and, in the end, they won.

Following my pact with the mountain—once I could move easily in the most forbidding places—I proposed to myself an agreement with the animals: horses, goats, birds. This was accomplished through the skin, by means of a sort of "touch" language, which I find difficult to describe now that my senses have lost the acuity of perception they possessed at the time. The fact remains that I could draw near animals where other human beings put them to precipitate flight. During a walk with Michel and Catherine, for instance, I ran forward to join a herd of horses. I was exchanging caresses with them when the arrival of Catherine and Michel caused them to scamper away.

All of this was taking place in June and July, and the refugees were piling up. Michel sent wire upon wire to my father in an effort to secure visas for Spain. Finally a cure brought a mysterious and very dirty piece of paper, coming from I know not what agent of my father's business connection, ICI (Imperial Chemicals), which should have allowed us to resume our journey. Twice already we had attempted to cross the Spanish border: the third attempt proved successful, thanks to the cure's bit of paper. Catherine and I reached Seo de Urgel. Unfortunately, Michel was unable to come over. The two of us then drove in the Fiat to Barcelona.

I was quite overwhelmed by my entry into Spain: I thought it was my kingdom; that the red earth was the dried blood of the Civil War. I was choked by the dead, by their thick presence in that lacerated countryside. I was in a great state of exaltation when we arrived in Barcelona that evening, convinced that we had to reach Madrid as speedily as possible. I therefore prevailed upon Catherine to leave the Fiat in Barcelona; the next day we boarded a train for Madrid.

The fact that I had to speak a language I was not acquainted with was crucial: I was not hindered by a preconceived idea of the words, and I but half understood their modern meaning. This made it possible for me to invest the most ordinary phrases with a hermetic significance.

In Madrid, we put up at the Hotel Internacional, near the railway station, leaving it later for the Hotel Roma. At the Internacional we dined that first night on the roof; to be on a roof answered for me a profound need, for there I found myself in a euphoric state. In the political confusion and the torrid heat, I convinced myself that Madrid was the world's stomach and that I had been chosen for the task of restoring this digestive organ to health. I believed that all anguish had accumulated in me and would dissolve in the end, and this explained to me the force of my emotions. I believed that I was capable of bearing this dreadful weight and of drawing from it a solution for the world. The dysentery I suffered from later was nothing but the *illness* of Madrid taking shape in my intestinal tract.

A few days later, in the Hotel Roma, I met a Dutch man, Van Ghent, who was Jewish and somehow connected with the Nazi government, who had a son working for Imperial Chemicals, the English company. He showed me his passport, infested with Swastikas. More than ever I aspired to ridding myself of all social constraints; to that end, I made a present of my papers to an unknown person and tried to give Max's passport to Van Ghent, but he refused to take it.

This scene took place in my room; the man's gaze was as painful to me as if he had thrust pins into my eyes. When he refused to take Max's passport, I remember that I replied: "Ah! I understand, I must kill him myself," i.e., disconnect myself from Max.

Not content with giving my papers away, I felt obliged to strip myself of everything. One evening, as I sat by Van Ghent on a cafe terrace watching the people of Madrid passing by, I felt that they were being manipulated by his eyes. At that moment, he pointed out to me that I was no longer wearing a small brooch I had purchased a few moments before as a badge of the sorrows of Madrid. Then he added: "Look in your handbag and you will find it there." True enough, the badge was there. To me this was a further proof of Van Ghent's nefarious power. Disgusted, I rose to my feet and entered the cafe, with the firm intention of distributing everything I carried in my bag to the officers who were there. Not one of them would accept. It seems to me that this whole scene took place in a very short time; however I suddenly found myself alone with a group of Requeté officers. Van Ghent had disappeared. Some of the men rose and pushed me into a car. Later, I was in front of a house, the windows of which were adorned with wrought-iron balconies, in the Spanish style. They showed me into a room decorated in Chinese style, threw me onto a bed, and after tearing off my clothes raped me one after the other.

I put up such a fight that they finally grew tired and let me get up. While I was trying to adjust my clothes in front of a mirror, I saw one of them open my bag and remove all of its contents. This action seemed absolutely normal to me, as did his sousing my head with a bottleful of eau de cologne.

This done, they took me somewhere near El Retiro, the big park, where I wandered about, lost, my clothes torn. Finally I was picked up by a policeman, who took me back to the hotel, where I telephoned Van Ghent, who was asleep—it was perhaps three o'clock in the morning. I thought that my story would change his attitude towards the people of the earth, but he became furious, insulted me, and hung up. I went up to my room and found on my bed some nightgowns belonging to Catherine, which the laundress had deposited there by mistake. I imagined that Van Ghent, acknowledging my power, had made amends and sent them to me as a present. It seemed indispensable to me to try on these nightgowns immediately. I spent the rest of the night taking cold baths and putting on nightgowns, one after the other. One was of pale green silk, another pink.

I was still convinced that it was Van Ghent who had hypnotized Madrid, its men and its traffic, he who turned the people into zombies and scattered anguish like pieces of poisoned candy in order to make slaves of all. One night, having torn up and scattered in the streets a vast quantity of newspapers which I believed to be a hypnotic device resorted to by Van Ghent, I stood at the door of the hotel, horrified to see people in the Alameda go by who seemed to be made of wood. I rushed to the roof of the hotel and wept, looking at the chained city below my feet, the city it was my duty to liberate. Coming down to Catherine's room, I begged her to look at my face; I said to her: "Don't you see that it is the exact representation of the world?" She refused to listen to me and put me out of her room.

Coming down into the lobby of the hotel, I found there, among other people, Van Ghent and his son, who accused me of madness, obscenity, etc.; no doubt they were frightened by my afternoon exploit with the newspapers. Thereupon I ran to the public garden and played there for a few moments in the grass, to the amazement of all passersby. An officer of the Falange brought me back to the hotel, where I spent the night bathing over and over again in cold water.

To me Van Ghent was my father, my enemy, and the enemy of mankind; I was the only one who could vanquish him; to vanquish him it was necessary for me to understand him. He gave me cigarettes—they were pretty scarce in Madrid—and one morning when I was particularly excited, it dawned on me that my condition was not solely due to natural causes and that his cigarettes were doped. The logical conclusion of this idea was to report Van Ghent's horrible power to the authorities and then proceed to liberate Madrid.

An accord between Spain and England seemed to me the best solution. I therefore called at the British Embassy and saw the Consul there. I endeavoured to convince him that the World War was being waged hypnotically by a group of people—Hitler and Co.—who were represented in Spain by Van Ghent; that to vanquish him it would suffice to understand his hypnotic power; we would then stop the war and liberate the world, which was "jammed," like me and Catherine's Fiat; that instead of wandering aimlessly in political and economic labyrinths, it was essential to believe in our metaphysical force and divide it among all human beings, who would thus be liberated. This good British citizen perceived at once that I was mad, and phoned a physician, Martinez Alonzo by name, who, once he had been informed of my political theories, agreed with him.

That day, my freedom came to an end. I was locked up in a hotel room, in the Ritz. I felt perfectly content; I washed my clothes and manufactured various ceremonial garments out of bath towels in preparation for my visit to Franco, the first person to be liberated from his hypnotic somnambulism. As soon as he was liberated, Franco would come to an understanding with England, then England with Germany, etc. Meanwhile, Martinez Alonzo, thoroughly puzzled by my condition, fed me bromide by the quart and begged me repeatedly not to remain naked when waiters brought me my food. He was panic-stricken and stultified by my political theories, and after a fifteen-day calvary, he withdrew to a seaside resort in Portugal, leaving me in the care of a physician-friend of his, Alberto N.

Alberto was handsome; I hastened to seduce him, for I said to myself: "Here is my brother, who has come to liberate me from the *fathers*." I had not enjoyed love since Max's departure and I wanted to very badly. Unfortunately Alberto, too, was a perfect fool and probably a scoundrel besides. In truth, I believe he was attracted to me, all the more so as he was aware of the power of Papa Carrington and his millions, as represented in Madrid by the ICI. Alberto would take me out, and once more I enjoyed some sort of temporary freedom. But not for long.

I called every day on the head of the ICI in Madrid; he soon got tired of my visits, most of all because I came to enlighten him on politics and denounced him, pell-mell with Papa Carrington and Van Ghent, as being petty, very petty, and pretty ignoble; and this to himself, his wife, his maids, the hotel servants, and anyone who would listen to me. He summoned a certain Dr. Pardo and encouraged me to enlighten him on the affairs of the world. I soon found myself a prisoner in a sanatorium full of nuns. This did not last long either; the nuns proved unable to cope with me. It was impossible to lock me up, keys and windows were no obstacles for me; I wandered all over the place, looking for the roof, which I believed my proper dwelling place.

After two or three days, the head of the ICI told me

that Pardo and Alberto would take me to a beach at San Sebastian, where I would be absolutely free. I came out of the nursing home and got into a car bound for Santander.... On the way, I was given Luminal three times and an injection in the spine: systemic anaesthesia. And I was handed over like a cadaver to Dr. Morales, in Santander.

I am afraid I am going to drift into fiction, truthful but incomplete, for lack of some details which I cannot conjure up today and which might have enlightened us. This morning, the idea of the egg came again to my mind and I thought that I could use it as a crystal to look at Madrid in those days of July and August 1940—for why should it not enclose my own experiences as well as the past and future history of the Universe? The egg is the macrocosm and the microcosm, the dividing line between the Big and the Small which makes it impossible to see the whole. To possess a telescope without its other essential half—the microscope—seems to me a symbol of the darkest incomprehension. The task of the right eye is to peer into the telescope, while the left eye peers into the microscope.

In Madrid, I had not yet known suffering "in its essence"; I wandered into the unknown with the abandon and courage of ignorance. When I gazed at posters in the streets, I saw not only the commercial and beneficent qualities of Mr. X's canned goods but hermetic answers to my queries as well—when I read AZAMON COMPANY or IMPERIAL CHEMICALS, I also read CHEMISTRY

AND ALCHEMY, a secret telegram addressed to myself in the guise of a manufacturer of agricultural
machinery. When the telephone rang or fell silent,
answering or refusing to answer me, it was the inner
voice of the hypnotized people of Madrid (there is no
symbol hidden here, I am speaking literally). When
seated at a table with other people in the lobby of the
Hotel Roma, I heard the vibrations of beings as clearly
as voices—I understood from each particular vibra-
tion the attitude of each towards life, his degree of
power, and his kindness or malevolence towards me.
It was no longer necessary to translate noises, physical
contacts, or sensations into rational terms or words. I
understood every language in its particular domain:
noises, sensations, colours, forms, etc., and every one
found a twin correspondence in me and gave me a
perfect answer. As I listened to the vibrations, with
my back to the door, I knew perfectly whether Catherine, Michel, Van Ghent, or his son was entering the
dining room. As I looked into eyes, I knew the masters and the slaves and the (few) free men.

I worshipped myself in such moments. I worshipped myself because I saw myself complete—I was
all, all was in me; I rejoiced at seeing my eyes become
miraculously solar systems, kindled by their own
light; my movements, a vast and free dance, in which
everything was ideally mirrored by every gesture, a
limpid and faithful dance; my intestines, which vi-
brated in accord with Madrid's painful digestion,
satisfied me just as much. At that time, Madrid was

singing "*Los ojos verdes*" (The Green Eyes), after a
poem by, I think, Garcia Lorca. Green eyes had always
been for me my brother's, and now they were those of
Michel, of Alberto, and of a young man from Buenos
Aires whom I had met in the train between Barcelona
and Madrid. . . . Green eyes, the eyes of my brothers
who would deliver me at last of my father. I was obsessed by two other songs: "*El barco velero*" (The Sail-
boat), which was to take me to the Unknown, and
"*Bei mir bist du schön*," which was sung in every language and which, I thought, was telling me to make
peace on earth.

I ceased menstruating at that time, a function
which was to reappear but three months later, in
Santander. I was transforming my blood into compre-
hensive energy—masculine and feminine, microcos-
mic and macrocosmic—and into a wine that was
drunk by the moon and the sun.

I now must resume my story at the moment I came
out of the anaesthesia (sometime between the nine-
teenth and twenty-fifth of August 1940). I woke up in
a tiny room with no windows on the outside, the only
window being pierced into the wall to the right that
separated me from the next room. In the left corner,
facing my bed, stood a cheap wardrobe of varnished
pine; to my right, a night table in the same style, with
a marble top, a small drawer, and, underneath, an
empty space for the chamber pot; also a chair; near
the night table was a door which, I was to learn later,
led to the bathroom; facing me, a glass door gave onto

a corridor and onto another door panelled with opaque glass, which I watched avidly because it was clear and luminous and I guessed that it opened into a room flooded with sunshine.

My first awakening to consciousness was painful: I thought myself the victim of an automobile accident; the place was suggestive of a hospital, and I was being watched by a repulsive-looking nurse who looked like an enormous bottle of Lysol. I was in pain, and I realised that my hands and feet were bound by leather straps. I learned later that I had entered that place fighting like a tigress, that on the evening of my arrival Don Mariano, the physician who was head of the sanatorium, had tried to induce me to eat and that I had clawed him. He had slapped and strapped me down and compelled me to absorb food through tubes inserted into my nostrils. I don't remember anything about it.

I tried to understand where I was and why I was there. Was it a hospital or a concentration camp? I asked the nurse questions, which were probably incoherent; she gave me richly negative answers in English with a very disagreeable American accent. Later I learned that her name was Asegurado (or "insured," in the commercial sense of the word), that she was German, from Hamburg, and had lived for a long time in New York.

I never was able to discover how long I had remained unconscious: days or weeks? When I became sadly reasonable, I was told that for several days I had acted like various animals—jumping up on the wardrobe with the agility of a monkey, scratching, roaring like a lion, whinnying, barking, etc.

Held by the leather straps, I said very politely to Frau Asegurado: "Untie me, please." She said mistrustfully: "Will you be good?" I was so surprised by her question that I remained disconcerted for a few moments and could not produce an answer. I had only meant to do good to the entire world, and here I was, tied down like a wild beast! I could not understand, I had no memory whatsoever of my violent outbursts, and it all seemed to be a stupid injustice which I could only explain by blaming it on some Machiavellian impulse on the part of my guardians. I asked: "Where is Alberto?" "He is gone."

"Gone?"

"Yes, gone to Madrid."

Alberto gone to Madrid ... impossible! "Where are we here—far from Madrid?"

"Very far ..."

And so on. I felt that I was drifting further and further away as the conversation went on, finally to find myself in some unknown and hostile country. She then told me that I was here for a rest. ... For a rest! Finally, by dint of gentleness and very subtle arguments, I persuaded her to unstrap me and I dressed, full of curiosity for what lay outside the room. I walked along the corridor without attempting to open the door with the opaque glass panels, and reached a small square hall with windows closely corseted with iron bars. I thought: A funny rest place! These bars are here to prevent me from going out. I will come close to that iron and convince it to give my freedom back to me.

I was studying the matter closely, hanging bat-wise from the bars with my feet, my back turned to the room, and I was examining the bars on all sides, from all angles, when someone jumped on me. Falling miraculously back on my feet, I found myself face to face with an individual with the expression and aspect of a mongrel dog. I learned later that he was a congenital idiot who boarded at Dr. Morales's. Being a charity case, he served as a watchdog at Villa Covadonga, a pavilion for the dangerously and incurably insane named after Don Mariano's daughter who died. I realised that any discussion with such a creature was perfectly useless. I therefore took prompt measures to annihilate him. Frau Asegurado watched the battle from the vantage point of an armchair.

I was superior to my adversary in strength, will-power, and strategy. The idiot ran away weeping, covered with blood and terribly punished with scratches. I was told later that he would have submitted to death rather than come near me after that fight.

After I had explained a thousand times that I only wanted to see the garden, Frau Asegurado finally consented to accompany me outside. The garden was very green despite the tufts of bluish vapour of the tall eucalyptus trees; before Covadonga lay an orchard of apple-laden trees. I realized that autumn had come and, the sun being low, that evening was drawing near.

I probably was still in Spain. The vegetation was European, the climate soft, the architecture of Covadonga rather Spanish. But I was not at all sure of this, and seeing later the strange morality and conduct of the people who surrounded me, I felt still more at sea, and ended believing that I was in another world, another epoch, another civilisation, perhaps on another planet containing the past and future and, simultaneously, the present.

My keeper always wanted me to sit on a chair like a good girl. I refused, because I simply had to solve "the problem" as quickly as possible. When I walked to the right or left, she would follow me. Finally I sat down under a bower and a young man dressed in a blue smock—José—appeared suddenly and watched me with interest. I was relieved when I heard him speak Spanish. So I was in Spain! I found him handsome and attractive. He and Frau Asegurado followed me when I walked towards Villa Pilar to examine that pavilion. (By looking at the map, you will see the respective positions of Villa Pilar, Radiografia, Covadonga, Amachu, and Abajo (Down Below); that will enable you to get your bearings.) It was a grey stone building with iron-barred windows. To my utter surprise someone, hiding behind the bars, yelled at me from the first storey: "Leonora! Leonora!"

I was overcome. "Who are you?"

"Alberto!"

Alberto! So he was there! I wondered how I could manage to rejoin him, but the half-hidden face I glimpsed was hideous and deformed. As a matter of fact this was a practical joke of the nurses, who had suggested it to a madman by the name of Alberto. Yet I was pleased by this incident, believing that I had been followed by Alberto, that I had not been betrayed by him, and that he was a prisoner like me.

I jumped with joy among the apple trees, sensing again the strength, the suppleness and beauty of my body. Soon a very short nurse, Mercedes, appeared in the alley running at top speed, followed by Moro, a black dog; behind her came, at a more leisurely pace, a tall fat man, also dressed in white. I recognized in him a powerful being and hastened to meet him, saying to myself: "This man holds the solution of the problem." When I drew near, I was disagreeably impressed: I saw that his eyes were like Van Ghent's, only still more terrifying. I thought: He belongs to the same gang and is possessed like the others, be careful! He was Don Luis Morales, Don Mariano's son.

Although I had approached just out of reach of his hands, he tried to grab me. I avoided his touching me, while staying close. At that moment José appeared and seized me. I defended myself honourably till another man came up—Santos—and joined in the fray. Don Luis had seated himself comfortably between two tree roots and enjoyed the show as the two men, José and Santos, threw me on the ground. José sat on

Portrait of Dr. Morales

my head and Santos and Asegurado tried to fasten down my arms and legs, which kept thrashing around. Armed with a syringe that she wielded like a sword, Mercedes stuck a needle into my thigh.

I thought it was a soporific and decided not to sleep. To my great surprise, I did not get sleepy. I saw my thigh swell around the puncture, till the bump grew to the size of a small melon.

Frau Asegurado told me they had induced an artificial abscess in my thigh; the pain and the idea that I was infected made it impossible for me to walk freely for two months. As soon as they loosened their grip, I threw myself furiously against Don Luis. I drew his blood out with my nails before José and Santos had a chance to drag me away. Santos choked me with his fingers.

At Covadonga, they tore my clothes off brutally and strapped me naked to the bed. Don Luis came into my room to gaze upon me. I wept copiously and asked him why I was kept a prisoner and treated so badly. He left quickly without answering me. Then Frau Asegurado appeared once more. I asked her several questions. She said to me: "It is necessary that you should know who Don Luis is; every night he comes and talks to you; standing on your bed, you answer him according to his will." I did not remember any of this. I swore to myself that, from that moment on, I would remain watchful day and night, that I would never sleep and would protect my consciousness.

I don't know how long I remained bound and

naked. Several days and nights, lying in my own excrement, urine, and sweat, tortured by mosquitoes whose stings made my body hideous—I believed that they were the spirits of all the crushed Spaniards who blamed me for my internment, my lack of intelligence, and my submissiveness. The extent of my remorse rendered their assaults bearable. I was not greatly inconvenienced by the filth.

In the daytime, I was watched over by Frau Asegurado; at night, by José or Santos. From time to time, José would put his cigarette in my mouth so that I could inhale a few puffs of tobacco smoke; once in a while he would wipe my body, which was always burning hot, with a moist towel. I was grateful to him for his care. A squinting maidservant (they called her Piadosa) brought me my food: vegetables and raw eggs, which she introduced into my mouth with a spoon, taking good care not to be bitten. I was fond of her and *I would not have bitten her*. I thought that Piadosa, which means pious, meant painful feet, and I felt sorry for her because she had walked so much.

At night especially I would study my situation. I examined the straps with which I was bound, the objects and the persons by whom I was surrounded, and myself. An immense swelling paralysed my left thigh, and I knew that by freeing my left hand, I could cure myself. My hands are always cold and the heat of my leg *had* to melt under the coolness of my hand, the pain and the swelling would disappear. I don't know how, but I did manage to achieve this sometime later,

and soon both the pain and the inflammation sub-
sided, as I had foreseen.

One night, as I lay awake, I had a dream: a bed-
room, huge as a theatrical stage, a vaulted ceiling
painted to look like a sky, all of it very ramshackle but
luxurious, an ancient bed provided with torn curtains
and cupids, painted or real, I no longer know which; a
garden very much like the one in which I had strolled
the day before; it was surrounded by barbed wire over
which my hands had made plants grow, plants which
twisted themselves around the strands of wire and,
covering them, hid them from sight.

The day after I had that vision, Don Luis came and
spoke to me. I meant to ask him for a bandage for my
thigh, but this immediately went out of my head. I
also meant to ask him where Alberto was, but that
also escaped from my mind and I found myself, un-
wittingly, in the midst of a political discussion. While
I talked, I was surprised to find myself once more in a
garden similar to the one I had dreamt about. We
were sitting on a bench in the sunshine and I was neat
and dressed; I was happy and lucid, I was saying,
among other things: "I can do anything, thanks to
Knowledge." He answered: "In that case, make me
the greatest physician in the world."

"Give me my freedom, and you shall be."

I also said: "Outside this garden, so green and so
fertile, there is an arid landscape; to the left, a mountain on top of which stands a Druidic temple. That
temple, poor and in ruins, is my temple, it was built

for me, also poor and in ruins; containing only some dry wood, it will be the place where I shall live, calling on you every day; then I shall teach you my Knowledge."

This was the exact meaning of my words. However, when I was allowed later to go out, I found no such temple and the countryside was altogether fertile.

The memory of Alberto and of my thigh suddenly came back to my mind. I at once found myself naked, miserable, and dirty on my bed, and Don Luis stood up to leave.

After that conversation, I sent him, through José, a triangle drawn on a piece of paper (I had had great difficulties obtaining pencil, paper, and permission to free my hands to draw it). That triangle, to my way of thinking, explained everything.

I have been writing for three days, though I had expected to deliver myself in a few hours; this is painful, because I am living this period all over again and sleeping badly, troubled and anxious as I am about the usefulness of what I am doing. However, I must go on with my story in order to come out of my anguish. My ancestors, malevolent and smug, are trying to frighten me.

During the whole time I was tightly tied to my bed, I had an opportunity to get acquainted with my strange neighbours; a knowledge which did not help me solve my problem, to wit: Where was I and why was I there? They came and watched me through the glass panel in my door. Sometimes they would come in and talk to me: the Prince of Monaco and Pan America, Don Antonio with his matchbox containing a small piece of excrement, Don Gonzalo pursued and tortured by the Archbishop of Santander, the Marquis da Silva with his giant spiders— he was drying out from a heroin addiction (he was also suffering from the same injection that had been given me, though the nurses claimed the swelling came from a spi-der bite)—who had been the intimate friend of Alfonso

XIII, and was also Franco's friend. The Marquis was powerful in the Requeté, the Carlist Party; he was very nice and gaga.

Observing in those gentlemen a certain extravagance, I inferred that they were all under the hypnotic influence of Van Ghent's gang and that this place was consequently some sort of prison for those who had threatened the power of that group; also that I, the most dangerous of all, was fated to undergo a still more terrible torture in order to be reduced better still and become like my companions in distress.

I thought that the Moraleses were masters of the Universe, powerful magicians who made use of their power to spread horror and terror. I knew by dint of divination that the world was congealed, that it was up to me to vanquish the Moraleses and the Van Ghents in order to set it in motion again.

After several days of enforced immobility, I noticed that my brain was still functioning and that I was not defeated; I believed that my cerebral power was superior to my enemies'.

One evening, as I was being watched over by José and Mercedes, I suddenly felt horribly depressed. I felt that I was being possessed by Don Luis's mind, that his domination was swelling within me like a giant automobile tyre, and I heard his vast and immense desire to *crush* the Universe. I was penetrated by all of this as by a foreign body. This was torture. I was convinced at this moment that Don Luis was absent (which was true) and I had but one idea: to profit by his absence to escape the unclean power of his being. He had given me his power, convinced that I could not contain it, sure that he was my antipode, sure that he could kill me just like an intravenous injection of some virulent poison. Weeping, I begged José and Mercedes to unstrap me and come with me to Madrid, far from this terrible man. They answered: "But it would not be practical to leave for Madrid naked!" José however unstrapped me, and I prepared my luggage (a very dirty bed sheet and a pencil) while reciting: "Liberty, Equality, Fraternity." I walked painfully as far as the vestibule, followed by my little cortege. My left leg was horribly painful.

Don Luis returned at that moment. I heard his car—and he entered, accompanied by two men, one of whom was supposedly a Mexican upon whom I later avenged myself in Portugal. I don't remember who the other one was.

I don't know how long we all stood there transfixed —I thought I was holding them still with my eyes. The Mexican was laughing, the others were petrified. It was Don Luis, I believe, who finally broke the spell. My attention having faltered for one second, José and Mercedes threw themselves upon me and dragged me forcibly to my room. A hellish half hour followed: I held José and Mercedes by their hands and could not let them go: we were stuck to each other by some overpowering force, no one could speak or move. By an effort of will I managed to detach my hands from theirs; everyone then set to talking at a terrifying rate of speed. Whenever I would get hold of their hands once more, silence reigned immediately and our glances would once more be riveted to each other. This lasted perhaps several hours. This seemed to me the result of an infernal joke on the part of Don Luis, whose purpose was to prove that if I wanted to fraternize with José and Mercedes, we would be physically joined together like Siamese twins, and that otherwise his power would take hold of me again to destroy me.

The next day must have been Sunday, for I still hear the sound of bells outside and the clatter of horses' hooves, which gave me a terrible nostalgia and a desire to run away. It seemed impossible to communicate with the outside world; I wondered who would help someone, dressed in a bed sheet and a pencil, to get to Madrid.

I had heard about several pavilions; the largest one was very luxurious, like a hotel, with telephones and unbarred windows; it was called Abajo (Down Below), and people lived there very happily. To reach that paradise, it was necessary to resort to mysterious means which I believed were the divination of the Whole Truth. I was meditating on the manner in which I could get there as rapidly as possible when I was warned by the arrival of Moro, the dog, of Don Luis's visit. His expression was so different from yesterday's that it seemed to me that the world had turned backwards; with the night, his usual self-possession had vanished; he was dishevelled, dirty, agitated, and behaved like a madman. With the aid of José and Santos,

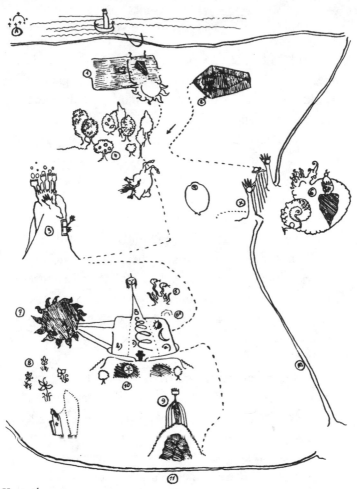

Key to the map

A. A desert scene, Covagonda cemetery
B. High wall surrounding the garden
X. Gate of the garden
1. Villa Covagonda
2. Radiography
3. Villa Pilar
4. Apple trees and the view of Casa
   Blanca and the valley
5. "Africa"
6. Villa Amachu
6b. Arbour

7. "Down Below"
8. Kitchen garden
9. Bower and cave
10. Don Mariano's "place"
11. "Outside World" Street
a. My room at "Down Below," the
   eclipse and the limbos
b. The lair
c. The library
   Wide "Down Below" alley

he removed all the furniture from my room except for the bed, from which I watched his strange activity. I knew that my clothes and a few small objects belonging to me were under lock and key in the wardrobe they were taking away. Frau Asegurado stood impassively next to me. I thought that the day of spring cleaning had arrived, that it heralded my liberation, and I was filled with joy. But once they had completely emptied the room, they left without giving me the slightest explanation.

Frau Asegurado told me that Don Luis had gone mad. I heard a great commotion above my room, accompanied by yells and insults. The dog, Moro, stood by my bed motionless and stared at the ceiling. I thought that it was Moro who, at that moment, held the power, that Don Luis had given himself up to a fit of raving madness in order to take a vacation from himself. I saw Frau Asegurado as a telephone cable who transmitted the will of Don Luis (Frau Asegurado was the most motionless of women).

I happened to be unstrapped that day, and from time to time I tried to escape, but Asegurado was watchful and I did not want to make use of violence against a woman for the sake of saving myself.

All day long the noise continued above my head, and I quietly rejoiced at the idea that Don Luis had become a raving maniac. Towards the end of that afternoon, the noise stopped suddenly and I heard steps on the stairs. I rushed into the hall, where a little old man appeared: it was Don Antonio with his matchbox, which still contained the sad little piece of excrement. I believed that Don Luis had sneaked into the old man's body: Don Antonio was not habitually violent and I have never been able to explain to myself the relentless noises of that strange Sunday.

After nightfall, Don Luis reappeared with a woman —Angelita: her street clothes, which were very neat, gave me some hope and I questioned her:

"You are a gypsy?" I asked.

"Yes."

"Where do you come from?"

"From Down Below."

"Is Down Below nice?"

"Delightful. Everyone is happy there."

"Take me with you."

"I can't."

"Why not?"

"Because you're not well enough to go there."

Thereupon Don Luis took me to the Sun Room, which was at that moment dark. I was entering that room for the first time. He began to talk about my visions, as though he had lived through them with me. Then he left suddenly; I wanted to follow him to Down Below with the gypsy, but Frau Asegurado prevented me and José came back to tie me down.

Later Piadosa got a bath ready for me. They bathed me for the first time that evening and cleaned my bed. I said to myself: "They are preparing my triumphal entry into Down Below." I believed they were purifying me in order to unite me with Alberto; I believed

that the palace had been made ready to receive me; I
believed this to be the dawn of freedom. Once I was
left alone, clean in my bed, strapped as usual, the small
window to the left lit up with such a beautiful warm
orange light that I felt a delightful presence next to
me. I was happy. Later José brought me his cigarette.

A new era began with the most terrible and blackest
day in my life. How can I write this when I'm afraid to
think about it? I am in terrible anguish, yet I cannot
continue living alone with such a memory... I know
that once I have written it down, I shall be delivered.
But shall I be able to express with mere words the
horror of that day?

The next morning, a stranger entered my room. He
carried in his hand a physician's bag of black leather.
He told me that he had come to take blood for a test
and that he had to be helped by Don Luis. I replied
that I was willing to receive one of them, but one at a
time only, for I had noticed that the presence of more
than one person in my room brought misfortune
to me; moreover, that I was going to leave for Down
Below and that I would not allow an injection to be
given to me under any pretext. The discussion lasted
for a pretty long time. It ended by my insulting him
and he went away. Don Luis then entered and I announced my departure to him. Gentle and insinuat-
ing, he began talking about the blood taking. I spoke
to him at length about my removal, about Alberto,

and other things I don't remember. We spoke eye to eye; he was holding my left hand. All of a sudden, José, Santos, Mercedes, Asegurado, and Piadosa were in my room. Each one of them got hold of a portion of my body and I saw the *centre* of all eyes fixed upon me in a ghastly stare. Don Luis's eyes were tearing my brain apart and I was sinking down into a well...very far... The bottom of that well was the stopping of my mind for all eternity in the essence of utter anguish.

With a convulsion of my vital centre, I came up to the surface so quickly I had vertigo. Once more I saw the staring, ghastly eyes, and I howled: "I don't want ...I don't want this unclean force. I would like to set you free but I won't be able to do so, because this astronomical force will destroy me if I don't crush you all...all...all. I must destroy you together with the whole world, because it is growing...it is growing, and the universe is not big enough for such a need of destruction. *I am growing. I am growing*...and I am afraid, because nothing will be left to destroy."

And I would sink again into panic, as if my prayer had been heard. Have you an idea now of what the Great Epileptic Ailment is like? It's what Cardiazol induces. I learned later that my condition had lasted for ten minutes; I was convulsed, pitiably hideous, I grimaced and my grimaces were repeated all over my body.

When I came to I was lying naked on the floor. I shouted to Frau Asegurado to bring me some lemons and I swallowed them with their rinds. Only she and

José were with me now. I rushed into the bathtub and splashed water all over me, on them both, on everything around me. Then I went back to bed, and tasted despair.

I confessed to myself that a being sufficiently powerful to inflict such a torture was stronger than I was; I admitted defeat, the defeat of myself and of the world around me, with no hope of liberation. I was dominated, ready to become the slave of the first comer, ready to die, it all mattered little to me. When Don Luis came to see me, later, I told him that I was the feeblest creature in the whole world, that I could meet his desires, whatever they were, and that I licked his shoes.

I must have slept for about twenty-four hours. I woke up in the morning; a little old man, dressed all in black, was watching me; I knew he was a master because the pinpoint pupils of his light eyes were similar to those of Van Ghent and Don Luis. This man was Don Mariano Morales. He spoke to me in French, very politely, something to which I was no longer accustomed.

"So you feel better, Mademoiselle?... I am no longer seeing a tigress, but a young lady."

He seemed to know me and I was expressing my surprise when Don Luis entered the room and said: "This is my father."

Don Mariano ordered that I be unstrapped and removed to the Sun Room in Covadonga. They could do what they pleased with me, I was as obedient as an ox.

The Sun Room was a pretty large room; one of its sides was made of opaque glass that gave out a dazzling light. Beatifically soaking in the muted sunshine, I felt as though I had left behind me the sordid and painful aspect of Matter and was entering a world which might have been the mathematical expression of Life. The room was furnished with a few chairs, a leather couch, and a small pinewood writing desk. The floor was covered with blue-and-white tiles. I lay down for hours in the light and contented myself with following the course of the sun through the glass panes. I took my food with docility and gave up resisting.

It was, I am almost certain of it, the night before I was injected with Cardiazol that I had this vision:

The place looked like the Bois de Boulogne; I was on top of a small ridge bordered with trees; at a certain distance below me, on the road, stood a fence like those I had often seen at the Horse Show; next to me, two big horses were tied together; I was impatiently waiting for them to jump over the fence. After long hesitations, they jumped and galloped down the slope. Suddenly a small white horse detached himself from them; the two big horses disappeared, and nothing was left on the path but the colt, who rolled all the way down where he remained on his back, dying. *I myself was the white colt.*

The terrible downfall induced by Cardiazol was followed by several rather silent days. Around eight in the morning, I would hear from a distance the siren of a factory, and I knew this was the signal for Morales and Van Ghent to call the *zombies* to work and also to wake me, I who was entrusted with the task of liberating the day. Piadosa would enter then with a tray on which stood a glass of milk, a few biscuits, and some fruit. I took in this food according to a special ritual:

First, I would drink the milk at one draught, sitting bolt upright in my bed.

Second, I would eat the biscuits, half reclining.

Third, I would swallow all the fruit, lying down.

Fourth, I would put in a brief appearance in the bathroom, where I would observe that my food went through without being digested.

Fifth, back in my bed, I would sit up again very straight and examine the remnants of my fruit, rinds and stones, arranging them in the form of designs representing as many solutions to cosmic problems. I believed that Don Luis and his father, seeing the problems solved on my plate, would allow me to go Down Below, to Paradise.

Frau Asegurado would come in for my bath and then would take me to the Sun Room. Here I was rid of all my familiar objects which, belonging to the troubled and emotional past, would have darkened my labours. Here I was alone and naked, with my bed sheet and the sun—the sheet united to my body in a dance. Here in the Sun Room I felt I was manipulating the firmament: I had found what was essential to solving the problem of Myself in relation to the Sun.

I believed that I was being put through purifying tortures so that I might attain Absolute Knowledge, at which point I could live Down Below. The pavilion with this name was for me the Earth, the Real World, Paradise, Eden, Jerusalem. Don Luis and Don Mariano were God and His Son. I thought they were Jewish; I thought that I, a Celtic and Saxon Aryan, was un-

dergoing my sufferings to avenge the José for the per-
secutions they were being subjected to. Later, with full
lucidity, I would go Down Below, as the third person
of the Trinity. I felt that, through the agency of the
Sun, I was an androgyne, the Moon, the Holy Ghost,
a gypsy, an acrobat, Leonora Carrington, and a woman.
I was also destined to be, later, Elizabeth of England.
I was she who revealed religions and bore on her
shoulders the freedom and the sins of the earth changed
into Knowledge, the union of Man and Woman with
God and the Cosmos, all equal between them. The
lump on my left thigh no longer seemed to form part
of my body and became a sun on the left side of the
moon; all my dances and gyrations in the Sun Room
used that lump as a pivot. It was no longer painful, for
I felt integrated into the Sun. My hands, Eve (the left
one) and Adam (the right one), understood each
other, and their skill was thereby increased tenfold.

With a few pieces of paper and a pencil José had
given me, I made calculations and deduced that the
father was the planet Cosmos, represented by the sign
of the planet Saturn:☺. The son was the Sun and I the
Moon, an essential element of the Trinity, with a microscopic knowledge of the earth, its plants and creatures. I knew that Christ was dead and done for, and
that I had to take His place, because the Trinity, minus
a woman and microscopic knowledge, had become
dry and incomplete. Christ was replaced by the Sun. I
was Christ on earth in the person of the Holy Ghost.

Three days perhaps after my second Cardiazol

injection, I was given back the objects which had been confiscated on my entering the sanatorium, and a few others besides. I realised that with the aid of these objects I had to set to work, combining solar systems to regulate the conduct of the World. I had a few French coins, which represented the downfall of men through their passion for money; those coins were supposed to enter into the planetary system as units and not as particular elements; should they join with other objects, wealth would no longer beget misfortune. My red-and-black refill pencil (leadless) was Intelligence. I had two bottles of eau de cologne: the flat one was the José, the other, cylindrical one, the non-José. A box of Tabu powder with a lid, half grey and half black, meant eclipse, complex, vanity, taboo, love. Two jars of face cream: the one with a black lid was night, the left side, the moon, woman, destruction; the other, with a green lid, was man, the brother, green eyes, the Sun, construction. My nail buff, shaped like a boat, evoked for me a journey into the Unknown, and also the talisman protecting that journey: the song "*El barco velero.*" My little mirror was to win over the Whole. As for my Tangee lipstick, I have but a vague memory of its significance; it probably was the meeting with colour and speech, painting and literature: Art.

Happy with my discovery, I would group these objects around each other; they wandered together on the celestial path, helping each other along and forming a complete rhythm. I gave an alchemical life to the objects according to their position and their contents. (My face cream Night, in the black-lidded jar, contained the lemon, which was an antidote to the seizure induced by Cardiazol.)

Lucid and gay, I waited impatiently for Don Luis. I said to myself: "I have solved the problems he set before me. I shall certainly be led Down Below." So I was horrified when, far from appreciating my labour, he gave me a second injection of Cardiazol.

Thereupon I organized my own defence. I knew that by closing my eyes, I could avoid the advent of the most unbearable pain: the stare of others. Therefore I would keep them closed for a very, very long time at a stretch. This was my expiation for my exile from the rest of the world; this was the sign of my flight from Covadonga (which for me was Egypt) and of my return Down Below (Jerusalem), where I was destined to bring Knowledge; I had spent too much time putting up with the solitude of my own knowledge.

Keeping my eyes closed enabled me to endure the second Cardiazol ordeal much less badly, and I got up very quickly, saying to Frau Asegurado, "Dress me, I must go to Jerusalem to tell them what I have learned." She dressed me and I went into the garden, meeting no obstacle, Frau Asegurado behind me. I followed the alley, between the trees, leaving the apple trees and Villa Pilar to the right. As I advanced everything became richer and more beautiful around me. I did not stop until I came to the door of Down Below. An old woman, Dona Vicenza, sister of Don Mariano, was coming out of the house with a glass of water and a lemon, which she handed to me. I drank the water and kept the lemon as a talisman with which to carry out my perilous mission. I reached the foot of the stairs in my Paradise with a dreadful anguish, an anguish wholly comparable to the one I had experienced in front of the mountain, in Andorra. But, as in Andorra, I once again found the strength to struggle against the invisible powers that were striving to detain me, and I triumphed.

There were three storeys: in each a door was open. I could see in the rooms, on the night tables, other solar systems as perfect and complete as my own. *"Jerusalem knew already!"* They had penetrated the mystery at the same time as I. On the third floor, I came upon a small ogival door; it was closed; I knew that if I opened it, I would be in the centre of the world. I opened it and saw a spiral staircase; I went up and found myself in a tower, a circular room lighted by five bull's-eye windows: one red, one green (the Earth and its plants), one translucent (the Earth and its men), one yellow (the Sun), and one mauve (the Moon, night, the future). A wooden column which served as an axis for this strange place jutted from the ceiling, passed through the centre of a pentagonal table, which was laid with a small, torn red tablecloth, covered with dust. I took the great disorder which reigned on this table for the handiwork of God and of His Son: disorder among the various objects that were there, disorder in the cogs of the human machinery which, immobilized, kept the world in anguish, war, want, and ignorance.

I still can see those objects very distinctly: two stout pieces of wood cut out in the shape of an enlarged keyhole—a small pink box containing gold powder—a number of laboratory saucers of thick glass, some crescent shaped, others half-moon shaped, the remainder perfectly round (I seem to remember that some were triangular)—an oblong tin on which were pasted labels bearing the name of Franco and containing a morsel of dirt—lastly, a metal disk and a medal of Jesus Christ. Attached to the wall, so as to form a triangle in this circular room, hung three rectangular tanks of a metal I was unable to identify, they were so dirty on the outside, while inside they were covered with a thick layer of paint. The first was mauve, another pink; I don't remember the colour of the third. Each one was pierced through its side with a hole through which passed the handle of a large spoon.

I began by laying down the disk next to the column and by placing on top of it the two pieces of wood (male and female). I then poured all the gold dust over them, thus covering the world with riches. I then placed the saucers inside the tanks, and the Jesus Christ medal and the Franco box in my pocket. I opened all the windows, as I would have opened those of Consciousness, except for one: the mauve-coloured one, the Moon's, since my "moon cycle," my menstrual period, had stopped. Having concluded the Work, I walked down the stairs and returned to "Egypt."

it was a wooden building, made me think of China—
halfway between Covadonga (Egypt) and Down Below (Jerusalem). I still had with me Piadosa, José, and
Frau Asegurado; and Don Luis had told me that he
did not believe it would be necessary to continue giving me Cardiazol. He had added: "This house will be
your own, your home and you will be responsible for
it." I, however, gave the word home a broader, cosmic
meaning, which was represented by the number six.

Despite the confidence Don Luis had placed in me,
despite the commonplace appearance of the small
bungalow, which aroused no mistrust in my mind, I
felt, upon entering the inner corridor that separated
the various rooms, as though I was caught in a laby-
rinth, like a rat. The doors in the corridor looked as if
they had been cut out of the wall and were part of it,
and became almost invisible when closed. So here I
was, confronted with a Chinese puzzle which I had to
solve with the knowledge secured in Egypt.

One day Don Luis announced to me the visit of
Nanny, who had been with me till my twentieth year.
She arrived in great exaltation, after a terrible fifteen-
day journey in the narrow cabin of a warship. She had
not expected to find me in an insane asylum and
thought she was going to see the healthy girl she had
left four years ago. I received her coldly and mistrustfully: she was sent to me by my hostile parents, and
I knew that her intention was to take me back to

them. Upset by my attitude, Nanny became nervous. Frau Asegurado considered her arrival a regrettable event, though not dangerous for me. Nanny was mortified and horribly jealous because another woman had taken her place by my side. For me their jealousy became a cosmic problem, an almost impossible task that I had to solve, at Home, Amachu. When I left with Frau Asegurado for the big garden, I would give Nanny some task to keep her indoors. This happened every morning, at eleven, according to ritual.

I would get ready to enter the gate of Paradise; from the threshold, we overlooked the entire estate and the valley; my joy was so complete that I would be compelled to halt for a few minutes and turn enraptured eyes toward a very green spot of grass where a small boy armed with a stick was watching over some cows. Then we would follow the wide alley leading to Down Below; we walked through a bower, in which I sat down; all around me was the Garden of Eden, to my left Don Luis's garage, where I always hoped to see him arrive. I would remain there, watchful and quiet, and allow Frau Asegurado to enter Down Below. She would come out a few moments later, laden with a tray on which stood a glass of milk, biscuits, honey, and a cigarette of blond tobacco: the food of the gods, which I savoured in ecstasy. I was beginning to get fatter. Then I would go into my dear Down Below; I would go straight across the hall to the library: this was a rectangular room furnished with a writing desk and a small bookcase. The room opened into two other rooms: one day when the door to the left stood ajar, I recognized the room from the vision I had had in Covadonga, a room with a vaulted ceiling, painted to represent the sky. Immediately I called it my room, the room of the Moon. The other room, the one to the right, was the room of the Sun, my Androgyne. I would sit at the desk after choosing a book by Unamuno in which he had written: "God be thanked: we have pen and ink." At that moment, Angelica, the Gypsy (in fact a nurse) who lived in Down Below, would bring me a pen and some paper. I would make out the horoscope of the day and entrust it to her, to give to Don Luis.

The library gave out onto a large terrace, where I would rest a moment. There, sitting above the Moraleses' dining room, I absorbed the atmosphere of Down Below. Then I would go down the stairs to the left, which led to the back part of the garden; on a mound stood a rather dilapidated bower; Frau Asegurado would bring me a chair and I would sit there, gazing at the valley over the iron gate, then set to work on the three figures which continually obsessed me: 6, 8, and 20; after lengthy calculations, I would get the figure 1600, which called to mind Queen Elizabeth.... I thought at the time that I was her reincarnation. I would then come down from my bower and go around the mound, behind which a sort of cave had been dug for garden tools. Dead leaves were heaped there, and in my mind the heap took the shape of a tomb, which became for me Covadonga's and my own.

One day, on the path along the back of the garden, I met Don Luis and I asked him if he wanted to go to China with me. He answered: "I do; but you mustn't say so to anybody, you talk too much. Learn to keep inside you the things that occupy your mind." (This was the signal for my first inhibition, my entry into hermetism.) Then he gave me a stick, which he called my Stick of Philosophy. It became a companion on all my walks.... Then I went into the garden, under the apple trees, and returned to Amachu in time for lunch.

In the evening, I would call on the Prince of Monaco, in Villa Pilar; we would listen together to Radio Andorra. I sat there happily as the Prince typed endless diplomatic letters at a furious rate. Whenever he stopped, we would exchange ideas with the utmost seriousness. His room was plastered with maps; the one that interested me particularly was a map of France and northern Spain on which my journey was traced in red pencil. I believed that the Prince was teaching me about my own journey.

Don Luis would call on me at midnight; his presence in my room at that hour inspired me with a desire for him. He talked to me gently and I believed he was coming to examine my delusions. Without waiting for his questions, I would say: "*I have no delusions*, I am playing. When will you stop playing with me?" He would stare at me in amazement at finding me lucid, then laugh. And I would say: "Who am I?" while thinking: Who am I *to you*?

He would leave without answering, completely disarmed.

In a moment of lucidity, I realised how necessary it was to extract from myself all the personages who were inhabiting me. But the determination to expel Elizabeth was the only need that remained with me: she was the character I disliked most of all. I conceived the idea of constructing her image in my room: a small, three-legged round table represented her legs; for a body, I placed a chair on top of the table and on that chair a decanter which represented her head. Into the decanter I stuck dahlias and yellow and red roses—Elizabeth's consciousness; then I dressed her up in my own clothes and placed on the floor, by the legs of the table, Frau Asegurado's shoes.

I had reconstructed this image so that it might leave me. I had to get rid of everything my illness had brought me, to cast out these personalities, and thus begin my liberation.

Happy with my success, I was on my way through the garden to Down Below when I noticed an enormous tuft of reeds which had grown in an old shell hole; spontaneously, I called the place Africa and set to gathering branches and leaves with which I completely covered myself. I returned to Amachu in a state of great sexual excitement. It seemed only natural to me to find Don Luis in my room, busy examining Elizabeth's dummy. I sat down next to him and he caressed my face and introduced his fingers gently into my mouth: This gave me real pleasure. Then he took my notebook and wrote down on one page: "*O Corte, o cortijo*" (You belong at court, or in a farmyard). Whereupon I took to wanting him terribly, and to writing him every day.

One day at lunch I was upset by a nauseous smell in my room—they were spreading manure on the neighbouring fields. I could not understand why God the Father should tolerate that my meals be poisoned. Indignant, I rose from the table and, followed by Frau Asegurado, proceeded to find Don Mariano in his own dining room. Don Luis turned to my nurse and addressed her in German; irritated because I could not understand what he was saying, jealous because he was talking *to her* and not to me, I sat down between the two of them. I observed very clearheadedly that I was being run through by an electric current that went from the one to the other. To make sure I stood up, drew away from them, and felt immediately that the current had left my body. I knew that this current was the fluid of the fear they both had of me.

Don Mariano gave me his permission to move, and this is how I was admitted into Down Below. Frightened by the idea of living in the big garden, where she was afraid of meeting madmen, Nanny tried to dissuade me from installing myself Down Below. It was, she said, a dangerous and evil place. I insisted so much that she ended by yielding.

I arrived at last in the room with the vaulted ceiling, which I had seen in a vision at the beginning of my illness. The room was just as I had seen it, only smaller, and the painted ceiling was in fact flat, not vaulted; I entered there without emotion, almost with a sense of disappointment. I was examining the windows attentively, for I wanted to make sure that no microphones had been attached to them, when a large dragonfly entered and sat on my hand, its feet clinging to my skin. Its wings were trembling, it clung to me as if it would never again detach itself. I spent several minutes looking at it in this way, holding my hand motionless, until the dragonfly fell dead onto the tiles of the floor....

That evening at dinnertime when I entered the circular dining room at Down Below, I was told that I could select my table; I realized that I had to find my place in the circle, and sat at 45 degrees to the left of the door, which seemed to me the place where I could best intercept all interesting currents in the room.

A few days later Don Luis proposed to me my first outing: we drove out in an automobile to pay some calls. We went to see a pregnant young lady to whom he had to give an injection (I believed it would be an injection of Cardiazol, and that I was the child she was bearing). She gave me a package of cigarettes and they left me alone in a dark drawing room. I rushed to the bookcase and found a Bible, which I opened at random. I happened on the passage in which the Holy Ghost descends upon the disciples and bestows upon them the power to speak all languages. I was the Holy Ghost and believed I was in limbo, my room—where the Moon and the Sun met at dawn and at twilight.

When Don Luis came in, accompanied by the young lady, she spoke to me in German and I understood her, though I do not know the language. She gave me the Bible, which I pressed under my arm, eager to return home and hold my Stick of Philosophy, which Don Luis had not allowed me to take along.

When I entered the library of my pavilion, I found Nanny armed with my Stick. She needed it, she said, to defend herself against the demented inmates. How could she expect to put to such use my dear companion, my surest means of Knowledge? At that moment I hated her.

My second ride was in a horse carriage. Don Luis took me to the undertaker's, in Santander, where he rented me a carriage pulled by a small black horse. A very small boy sat down next to me, to keep me company. I drove the horse very fast and finally attained what felt like a dizzy speed, while the excited child cried out: "Faster! Faster!" In a wide avenue, we caught up with a company of soldiers who were singing: "Ay, ay, ay, no to mires en el rio" (Don't look at yourself in the river). I returned, convinced that I had accomplished an act of the utmost importance.

One morning, Don Luis advised me to start reading. He gave Frau Asegurado a list of books and told her to take me to the bookstore. I was quiet and very happy before such a quantity of books, among which I expected to be allowed to choose freely. But I felt my hand reach in the opposite direction to the one I intended, and pick up books I had absolutely no desire to read. At that moment I noticed Frau Asegurado standing behind me; she felt to me like a *vacuum cleaner*. Every time I got a book off the shelves, I would consult the list, hoping that its title would not be there: but there I would find it every time. I begged her to leave my brain alone, demanded the freedom of my own will. I returned home in a rage. Frau Asegurado remained passive, unmoved, as if withdrawn from the scene. Don Luis showed up in my room immediately upon my return. I yelled at him: "I don't accept your force, the power of any of you, against me; I want my freedom to act and think; I hate and reject your hypnotic forces." He took me by the arm and led me to a pavilion which was not in use.

"I am the master here."

"I am not the public property of your house. I, too, have private thoughts and a private value. I don't belong to you."

And suddenly, I burst into tears. He took me by the arm, then, and I realised with horror that he was going to give me my third dose of Cardiazol. I promised him all that it was within my power to give if only he would desist from giving me the injection. On the way, I picked up a small eucalyptus fruit, in the belief that it would help me. He took me, vanquished, to the radiography pavilion. I resigned myself to take the place of his sister, to undergo the last ordeal, the one that would give him back Covadonga in my own person.

The room was papered with painted, silvery pine

trees on a red background; a prey to the most complete panic, I saw pine trees in the snow. In the midst of convulsions, I relived my first injection, and felt again the atrocious experience of the original dose of Cardiazol: absence of motion, fixation, horrible reality. I did not want to close my eyes, thinking that the sacrificial moment had come and determined to oppose it with all my strength.

I was then taken to Down Below in a cataleptic state. Tirelessly, Nanny repeated, "What have they done to you...what have they done to you?" and wept by my bed, thinking that I was dead. But, far from being touched by her sorrow, I was exasperated by it, for I felt at that moment that my parents were still trying to pull me back through her. I drove her away; but from the next room, where one withdrew, I still suffered this suction of their will. I knew when she went away. At last I entered painlessly that state of prostration that usually follows this kind of treatment. Don Mariano was at my bedside when I woke up. He advised me not to return to my parents. At that moment, I regained my lucidity. My cosmic objects, my night creams and nail buff, had lost their significance.

It was at this time that Etchevarría appeared. I was sitting in the garden when another inmate, Don Gonzalo, advanced toward me and gave me a book from a man named Etchevarría, who sent apologies for being unable to bring it in person, as he was ill in bed that day. Two days later, I met in the library a small man with a grey face, wrapped in warm clothes. This was

Etchevarría. He spoke amiably about my country. He sat down in the dining room at a table next to mine, then gazed at me for a long time, kindly, and said at last: "You will not remain here long."

A feeling of joy slowly grew within me: I was talking with a reasonable man who inspired no fear, who took me seriously and sympathetically. I spoke to him of my power over animals. He answered without a trace of irony: "Power over animals is a natural thing in a person as sensitive as you are." And I learned that Cardiazol was a simple injection and not an effect of hypnotism; that Don Luis was not a sorcerer but a scoundrel; that Covadonga and Amachu and Down Below were not Egypt, China, and Jerusalem, but pavilions for the insane and that I should get out as quickly as possible. He "demystified" the mystery which had enveloped me and which they all seemed to take pleasure in deepening around me.

After long conversations about desire, Etchevarría advised me to have sex with José. I ceased then being interested in Don Luis and began desiring José. I would meet him in various secluded spots of the garden and, spied on by Frau Asegurado and Mercedes, we would exchange quick and uncomfortable kisses. José was very fond of me. He plied me with cigarettes....

He cried when I went away.

Postscript

I had a cousin in Santander, in the other hospital, the big, ordinary hospital. He was a doctor, Guillermo Gil, and I think he was related to the Bamfords, my grandmother's family in Cheshire. He was half English and half Spanish. It was a coincidence. He arrived, and they didn't want anyone to see me. But he was a doctor and he insisted, and so I had an interview with him, and he said, "I'd like you to have tea with me. They can't refuse." Which they couldn't. And we chatted, and at the end, he said, "I'm going to write to the ambassador in Madrid, and get you out." Which he did. They sent me to Madrid with Frau Asegurado, my keeper.

It was New Year's Eve, I remember it very well. It was extremely cold, and we got held up in Avila, where Santa Teresa was born. There was a long train with many trucks full of sheep, and they were all crying from the cold. It was awful, the Spanish can be so terrible with animals. I'll remember the suffering sheep to my dying day. It was like Hell. We were held up, I don't know why, for hours, listening to this absolutely hellish lament, and I was alone with Frau Asegurado.

Then we arrived in Madrid, and were staying in a large, rather expensive hotel. It is sort of tricky to talk about this period, because Imperial Chemicals were really up to all kinds of things. The man who ran it reappeared, and he was allowed to take me out to lunch, without Frau Asegurado, and sometimes in the evening too. One night, he and his wife had me to dinner, and they were afraid of me, because I'd just come out of the madhouse. I could see she was hesitating to give me a knife and fork. It was all I could do not to crack up, it was so funny. She was absolutely petrified of me; they both were. Then she didn't want to see me again. I was much too alarming to have around in the social life of Madrid.

One night it was very windy—this was winter, remember, and it's very cold in Madrid then—I went with him to a very expensive restaurant, and he said, "Your family have decided to send you to South Africa, to a sanatorium where you'll be very happy because it's so lovely there."

I said, "I'm not sure about that."

He added, "I have another idea, personal, of course: I could give you a lovely apartment here, and I could see you very very often." And he grabbed my thigh.

So I was then in front of a huge decision. Either I was shipped to South Africa, or I was going to bed with this appalling man. I quickly went to the lavatory. But I still hadn't decided when I came out. We were about to leave the restaurant when there was a tremendous gust of wind and the metal sign of the restaurant fell just in front of me, at my feet. It could have killed me, and so I turned around to him, and I said, "No. It's no." And that's all I said. I didn't have to say any more than that.

"It's going to be Portugal and then South Africa for you then," he said.

They got everything ready to send me off, and Frau Asegurado went back to Santander. I was put on the train, with my papers, whatever they were. I'd given them all away but they seemed to turn up again. I was being shipped out. They were ashamed of me.

I was telling myself, "I'm not going to South Africa and another sanatorium!" Yet it didn't occur to me to get off the train before getting to Lisbon.

I descended in Lisbon, and was met by a committee from Imperial Chemicals—two men who looked like policemen, and a very very hard-faced woman. They said, "You're very lucky, you're going to live in a lovely house in Estoril, with Mrs. Whatever-Her-Name."

I'd learned by then, You don't fight with such people. You have to think more quickly than they. So I said, "That will be lovely."

We arrived in a house in Estoril, a few miles from Lisbon. There was barely a half inch of bathwater and a lot of parrots. I spent the night there and I did a bit of hard thinking, and the next day I said, "The weather's going to be terrible for my hands. I must have some gloves. And I haven't got a hat."

I was thinking, Get to Lisbon. It worked. She said, "Of course you must. Nobody goes out without gloves."

So off we went. We reached Lisbon, and I said to myself, "Now or never." I had to find a café that looked big enough, and then, "Aargh!" I cried, clutching my stomach. "Got to go to the bathroom." "Yes, immediately," she said. She conducted me inside. I had judged correctly: it was a café with two doors. I nipped out, got a taxi—I must have had a bit of money for buying the gloves—and I told the driver, in Spanish, "Mexican Embassy."

I'd met Renato Leduc, again, in Madrid. I'd run into him at a thé dansant. I was allowed to watch the other people dancing, though I wasn't allowed to dance, of course. I was with my keeper, Frau Asegurado—I knew Renato from Paris. He was a friend of Picasso—I told him what had happened, and I asked, "Where are you going, for God's sake?" We had to talk in shorthand in French, which she didn't speak. Renato told me then, Lisbon.

So I landed at the Mexican consulate and there were a bunch of Mexicans I'd never seen. I asked them if Renato was there, and they said, No, they didn't know when he'd be in. I told them I was going to stay and wait. They protested, "Señorita, but..." This and that. So I said, "The police are after me." Which was more or less true. So they said, "In that case..." Wink, wink. "You can wait for Renato."

The ambassador was wonderful with me later. I must have gone in to see him, and he said, "You're on Mexican territory. Even the English can't touch you." I don't know when Renato appeared. Eventually, he said, "We're going to have to get married. I know it's awful for both of us, as we don't believe in this sort of thing, but…" At that time I was as frightened of my family as of the Germans. I'd found Renato attractive when I first met him, and I still found him very attractive. He had a dark face like an Indian's and very white hair. No, I felt perfectly sane. I was just feeling that I would do anything not to be sent to Africa, not to fall in with my family's plans.

Then Max appeared, with Peggy [Guggenheim] and we were always together, all of us. It was a very weird thing, with everybody's children, and ex-husbands and ex-wives. I felt there was something very wrong in Max's being with Peggy. I knew he didn't love Peggy, and I still have this very puritanical streak, that you mustn't be with anyone you don't love. But Peggy is very maligned. She was rather a noble person, generous, and she never ever was unpleasant. She offered to pay for my airplane to New York, so I could go with them. But I didn't want that. I was with Renato, and eventually, we went by boat to New York, where I stayed for almost a year, until we left for Mexico.

That was the story.

My mother came to Mexico when my son Pablo was born in 1946. But we never talked about this time. It's the sort of thing English people of that generation didn't discuss. That was one side of my mother's peculiar and rather complex character.

One would have thought they would have come themselves to Santander. But you know, they didn't.

Nanny was sent. You can imagine how much Spanish Nanny talked. It's a wonder she ever got there. What is terrible is that one's anger is stifled. I never really got angry. I felt I didn't really have time. I was tormented by the idea that I had to paint, and when I was away from Max and first with Renato, I painted immediately.

I never saw my father again.

As told to Marina Warner
July 1987, New York

Note on the Text

First written in English in 1942 in New York (text now lost). Dictated in French to Jeanne Megnen in 1943, then published in *VVV*, No. 4, February 1944, in a translation from the French by Victor Llona. The original French dictation was published by Editions Fontaine, Paris, 1946. Both the French dictation and the Victor Llona translation were used as the basis for the text here, which was reviewed and revised for factual accuracy by Leonora Carrington in 1987.

OTHER NEW YORK REVIEW CLASSICS

For a complete list of titles, visit www.nyrb.com or write to:
Catalog Requests, NYRB, 435 Hudson Street, New York, NY 10014

* *Also available as an electronic book.*